Chicken

& Other Birds

From the perfect roast chicken to Asian-style duck breasts

Paul Gayler MBE

jacqui
small

Photographs by Kevin Summers

CONTENTS

First published in 2015 by
Jacqui Small LLP
An imprint of Aurum Press
74–77 White Lion Street
London N1 9PF
Copyright © 2015 text by Paul Gayler
Photography, design and layout
copyright © 2015 Jacqui Small

Publisher: Jacqui Small
Managing Editor: Emma
  Heyworth-Dunn
Art Direction & Design:
  Lawrence Morton
Editor: Hilary Mandleberg
Photographer: Kevin Summers
Prop Stylist: Cynthia Inions
Production: Maeve Healy

ISBN: 9781909342507
A catalogue record for this book
is available from the British Library.
2015 2014 2013
10 9 8 7 6 5 4 3 2 1
Printed in China

INTRODUCTION

In the nineteenth century, gastronome Brillat-Savarin wrote that 'poultry is for the cook what canvas is for the painter'. I couldn't agree more. It is the simple, mild flavours of poultry that make it so extremely versatile.

Nearly every culture around the world has at least one way of preparing its poultry, incorporating the flavours and cooking methods that are unique to that culture's particular food heritage and local culinary styles.

I am thrilled to have brought together in this book some of my favourite poultry recipes. Some are classics that have withstood the test of time, some are great recipes that I have sourced from all over the globe, and some are recipes that I first prepared many years ago when I was a young trainee chef.

Although most of these recipes are based on chicken, there are also many for other types of poultry. But one of the beauties of poultry is its adaptability, so if you fancy a dish using guinea fowl or duck, it is simply a matter of replacing the chicken in the recipe with your choice of poultry, and adjusting the cooking time according to the size and type of the bird or the cut. The opportunities for variety are endless – and are in your own hands.

As I am sure you are all too well aware, battery hen houses and intensive breeding techniques have brought poultry prices down considerably in recent years. Poultry is now relatively inexpensive and commonplace. Before that, it was the preserve of the rich or was only eaten on special occasions.

But these intensive faming methods have their critics. We have now moved into a more health-conscious era where many people are unhappy with the idea of raising our poultry and meat using hormones, antibiotics and other chemicals. Chefs and much of the public now generally prefer the use of free-range or organic poultry and meat, though, of course, many people still like to buy cheaper, intensively bred products.

We all have a choice. Supermarkets are very cost-sensitive and continue to offer cheaper products for those that want them. Sceptics have yet to be convinced that the extra costs involved in producing free-range or organic poultry and meat are worthwhile.

But I am going to get on my high horse and plead for the virtues of buying the best you can afford. As far as I am concerned, the extra costs are worth every penny. The free-range, organic poultry you buy will be better in every way; in fact, I guarantee that it will be a revelation. The texture will be slightly firmer than the cotton-wool texture we have come to expect from our poultry but more importantly, the flavour will be far superior – richer and gamier.

What is more, if the demand grows for well-reared, free-range and organic poultry, the cheaper it will become and the better it will be for the welfare of the birds.

For me, 'real food' wins every time and even the best poultry still offers great value. It can be cooked in so many ways. You can roast it with butter and fresh herbs, you can skewer and grill (broil) it, you can poach it gently in a light, creamy sauce, use it in slow-casseroled dishes, add it to tasty salads, or coat it in breadcrumbs and deep-fry it to a delicious crispness.

Whatever your taste, you will find a recipe here to enjoy. Chicken and all its poultry cousins rarely lets you down. I hope you enjoy this book and the recipes I want to share with you.

Bon appétit.

GETTING TO KNOW YOUR BIRDS

Most of us automatically shop for chicken. It's the easiest type of poultry to find, it's relatively inexpensive and it's available all year round. But nowadays we're extremely lucky to have a wider range of birds at our disposal than ever before. Go to any good butcher and poulterer and you can choose from turkey, duck, goose, guinea fowl, squab pigeon and quail. So start here and learn what each type of bird has to offer and what to look for when shopping. Become familiar with how to handle and store your poultry, and how to prepare it for the oven. I hope you'll soon be feeling more adventurous.

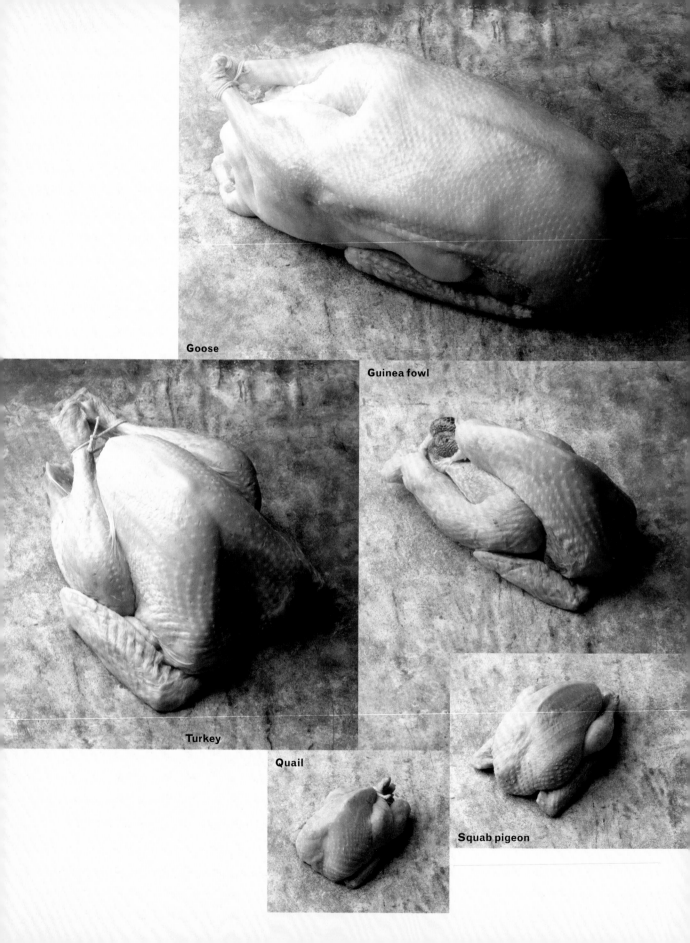

Goose

Guinea fowl

Turkey

Quail

Squab pigeon

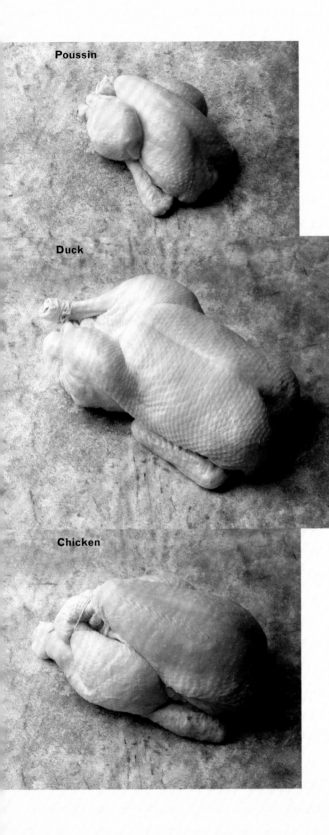

Poussin

Duck

Chicken

The variety of poultry

CHICKEN

Chicken is the most common and most popular poultry the world over. The way it is prepared is, of course, sometimes determined by region and culture. Chicken is believed to be a descendant of the red jungle fowl that was raised centuries ago in northern parts of the Indian sub-continent.

The most commonly available meat in Britain in the Middle Ages, its popularity grew steadily and consumption of this versatile poultry increased even more in Britain after the Second World War. In fact, sales of chicken in Britain overtook those of beef in the early 1990s after the BSE (Bovine spongiform encephalopathy) scare.

Nowadays, Britain boasts some of the best-reared chicken in the world. British breeds include, for example, the Label Anglais, produced in Essex, the Creedy Carver of Devon, and the Suffolk and the Sussex. All these varieties are specialist-reared and have a flavour that many consider to compare favourably with the famous Poulet de Bresse and Landes breeds from France. As with most poultry, the females produce the most flesh.

Chicken adapts well to virtually every cooking method, from the intense, high heat of roasting and barbecuing to slow braising and poaching, which produce a softer, mellower flavour.

TURKEY

Turkey is low in fat, which makes it a good choice if you are trying to eat a low-fat diet. Brought to Europe from Mexico during the Spanish conquests of the sixteenth century, turkey had been prized for centuries by the Aztecs and soon became popular throughout Europe.

Although you can buy turkey breasts nowadays, the most popular way it is sold is as a whole bird, making it is ideal for large family gatherings.

In Britain, a plump roasted turkey filled with classic chestnut stuffing, remains the highlight of the traditional Christmas dinner, while in the United States, roast turkey with cranberries still adorns most Thanksgiving tables.

It is fair to say that turkey has never really proved popular during the rest of the year, which is a great shame. If it is cooked properly and with care, it can be prepared in many delicious ways, as you will find in this book.

There are three main varieties of turkey in Britain – the common white, the black and, my favourite, the bronze, which has a gamier flavour and a delectable taste. In the United States, heritage turkeys – raised according to historic methods, and with darker meat and a gamier flavour than standard broad-breasted, white turkeys – are king. Heritage turkeys consist of ten specific breeds, including Nargansett, Bourbon Red and White Holland. For the best flavour, choose a hen bird every time.

DUCK AND GOOSE

Goose and duck fat are great for roasting potatoes, but there's more to these birds than their fat. Many breeds of duck are reared for the table, from the wonderful Rouen and Nantes ducks of France to the British Gressingham, Aylesbury and Goosnargh breeds. In the United States, Long Island and Peking ducks are the most sought-after, while Muscovy ducks are gaining in popularity. And of course, in China, Peking duck is famous as the duck used in the eponymous dish.

The term 'duck' actually applies to birds that are more than eight weeks old; younger ducks are 'ducklings'. I think those with the best flavour are about 12 weeks old. By that age they have a deeper, richer flavour, especially when they are slow-roasted or braised.

Duck freezes well because of its high fat content. As well as being sold whole, it is available as portions and as boneless breasts.

Before the popularity of turkey in Europe, goose was often the bird of choice, especially for festive occasions. It remains very popular in Scandinavia and in central and northern Europe.

Most geese are at their prime for the table at about 6–9 months; at this stage they will weigh 4–6kg (8lb 13oz–12lb). After that they become tougher, fattier and require much longer cooking.

Choose a young bird with a pliable breastbone and a plump, well-filled breast. A young goose (gosling) will weigh 2–3kg (4½–6½lb) but the meat yield will be very small.

The French are the most enterprising when it comes to goose. They use the giblets for making sausages, the fat for cooking (goose fat in south-west France is what butter is to Normandy and olive oil is to Provence), and of course, there is the famous foie gras, made from goose liver.

The French also excel at preparing duck breasts and legs separately in the form of duck confit (see p.162). This helps to overcome the problem with duck (and with goose) of the legs remaining underdone when the bird is roasted, while the breast is cooked to beautiful pink perfection.

GUINEA FOWL AND SQUAB PIGEON

Guinea fowl are native to Africa; it is believed to have been the Greeks who first brought them to Europe. They are equivalent in size to small spring chickens but with dark-coloured meat and a flavour akin to chicken, though with a mild hint of game.

If not roasted with care, guinea fowl have a tendency to be a little dry, so they require regular basting. Some chefs like to place a few rashers (slices) of bacon on the breast or to smear a little butter under the skin to prevent the bird from drying out. I suggest cooking them slowly and at a lower temperature (see p.24). Older fowl are best braised or casseroled.

There are several breeds of domestic pigeon, or squab pigeon; these should not be confused with their wild relatives, the wood pigeons, which have a stronger gamey flavour, dark meat and a firmer texture. Squab pigeons are generally milk-fed, pale-fleshed and mellow in flavour. They are considered a real delicacy, especially in France. Killed at around four weeks, young birds are usually roasted, sautéed, griddled or grilled (broiled). They do not need to be hung. Older birds are often slow-braised or made into pies.

QUAIL

Quails are thought to have originated in Africa or China. They produce a deeply flavoured, highly sought-after meat that is slightly sweet and gamey in taste. They are also the smallest poultry birds. Unless you can find a larger specimen, you will generally need two birds per person.

They must be eaten fresh, usually within 36 hours of being killed. They are delicious roasted, fried or grilled (broiled), and their small eggs are also a prized delicacy and are now becoming widely available.

POULTRY BUYING GUIDE

When it comes to buying poultry, a good butcher will always be your best ally. I always prefer to buy my poultry free range from a traditional family butcher, or failing that, from the chilled meat counter of a good supermarket. The cost will be a little higher than buying intensively farmed, massed-produced poultry, but the flavour will be immeasurably better.

Always look for plump, healthy, clean birds with creamy, slightly pinkish skin and a fresh appearance. Check that the skin of whole birds or joints is intact and not torn in any way, and be wary of bruises, brown spots and any greenish patches on the surface.

Poultry can be purchased whole, cut into quarters or cut into breasts, legs, thighs or drumsticks. Buying a whole bird is cheaper than buying individual cuts: two breasts will cost nearly as much as a whole bird, whereas if you buy a whole bird, you can cut whatever size pieces you want, and you will also have the carcass for making stock. Purchasing chicken breasts is the most expensive way to buy chicken, whereas chicken in general is relatively inexpensive.

You also have the choice of buying your poultry fresh, chilled or frozen, but as far as I am concerned, buying frozen poultry is always a last resort. (In Britain, turkey is generally only available fresh at Christmas time: at other times of the year, you may only be able to find frozen turkey in the shops.)

Most chickens are now reared under strictly controlled conditions and on standardised diets that are designed to put on maximum flesh in minimum time. The result is that most birds are uniformly young and tender. Choosing one in preference to another is usually merely a matter of weight. Here is my guide to buying all sorts of poultry.

CHICKEN

Roasting chicken
also known as spring chicken
1.6–2.25kg (3lb 3oz–5lb)
serves 4

Breast
allow 170–180g (6–scant 6½oz)
per person

Thighs
allow 2–3
per person

Drumsticks
allow 2–3
per person

Double poussin
800–1kg (1¾–2¼lb)
serves 1

Single poussin
450–600g (1–1lb 5oz)
serves 1

DUCK

Whole duck
1.8kg (4lb)
serves 4

Breast
170–180g (6–scant 6½oz)
serves 1

Legs
allow 1 per person

GOOSE

Whole goose
4–6kg (8lb 13oz–12lb)
serves 6–8

GUINEA FOWL

Whole guinea fowl
1.5kg (3lb 3oz)
serves 4

Breast
160–170g (5½–6oz)
serves 1

Legs
allow 1 per person

SQUAB PIGEON

Whole squab pigeon
450–550g (1–1¼lb)
serves 1

TURKEY

Whole turkey
6–10kg (12–22lb)
The smaller size is good for an average family
serves 4–6

Handling and storing poultry

Poultry needs to be refrigerated as soon as possible after purchasing and ideally you should store it in the coldest part of the fridge, on the lowest shelf. Remove the giblets from whole birds before refrigerating.

Do not allow poultry to come into contact with or drip onto other foods, especially prepared, ready-to-eat foods, since it can contaminate them with harmful bacteria. Eat on the day of purchase or within 1–2 days.

To store cooked poultry, cool it and store it in the fridge, covered, for no longer than 1–2 days. When reheating cooked poultry, always ensure it is heated through thoroughly.

If you are freezing poultry, remove any giblets prior to freezing. To defrost frozen poultry, I recommend you defrost it as slowly as possible, overnight in the fridge. Large birds may even require two days. Thawing it too rapidly can be extremely hazardous and can increase the risk of food poisoning.

Always wash your hands thoroughly before and after handling poultry and clean your work surfaces, chopping (cutting) boards and knives thoroughly after use.

PREPARING POULTRY FOR COOKING

Oven-ready birds need very little preparation. If necessary, trim off any stubby feathers, remove the giblets from the cavity if you haven't already done so, then wipe the bird dry with kitchen paper, both inside and outside.

In general, if the recipe allows, I prefer to cook chicken with its skin on. The skin contains a lot of flavour and leaving it on helps to keep the flesh beneath moist and succulent.

To remove the skin, if the recipe requires it, simply loosen the skin with your fingers, then pull it off. It should peel off quite easily.

Larger birds such as geese contain lots of fat glands under the skin. Before cooking, prick the skin to allow the fat to drain (see p.48).

Before jointing or roasting poultry whole, first remove the wishbone located near the neck cavity. This makes it a great deal easier to joint the bird or carve it after roasting.

Cutting poultry into four joints

All you need to cut up a young whole bird are a sharp cook's knife and a chopping (cutting) board.

01 First remove the wishbone (see trussing a bird ready for roasting, p.17), then remove the winglets and the wings.
02 Cut down through the skin between the leg and the breast.
03 Bend the leg outwards to locate the hip joint.
04 Cut down through the joint to remove the whole leg – the drumstick with its thigh. French trim both drumsticks (see p.16).
05 French trim the breasts, then remove these from the carcass.
06 You will now have four main pieces – two breast joints and two leg joints, plus two wings and two winglets.

Cutting poultry into eight joints

First remove the wishbone (see trussing a bird ready for roasting, p.17), then remove the winglets and the wings and cut the chicken into four joints (see above).

07 Cut the leg joints further by cutting through the thigh bone to divide the thigh from the drumstick.
08 Cut the breast joints further by holding the wing joint and cutting diagonally towards the wing. This will yield two pieces from each breast.
09 You will now have eight main pieces – two thighs, two drumsticks, four breast portions, plus two wings and two winglets.

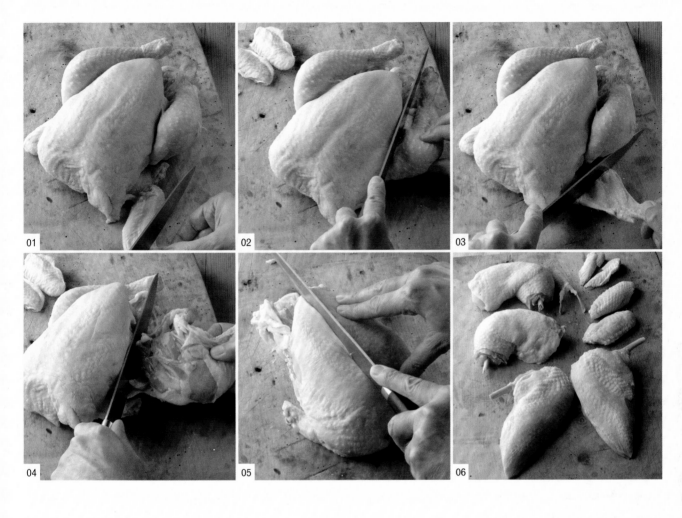

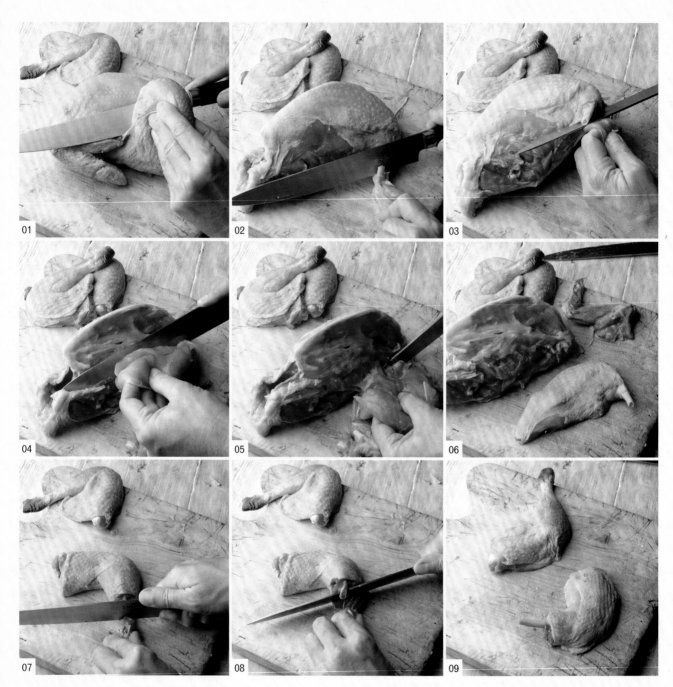

Preparing a bird French-trim style

01 **Place the bird on a large board and remove the whole leg – the drumstick with its thigh.**

02 **Run a knife around the end of the wing, hit the wing bone with a heavy cook's knife to break it, then cut around the wing to remove the wing and reveal some of the bone.**

03 **Scrape the flesh from the revealed wing bone.**

04 **Cut through the joint between the wing and the breast.**

05 **Cut the breast away.**

06 **Each breast will have part of the wing bone attached, giving it its French trim.**

07 **Return to the legs. Run a knife along the leg bone up to the knuckle to expose the bone. Cut about 2.5cm (1in) down from the knuckle and hit the leg bone with a heavy cook's knife to break it. Remove the knuckle.**

08 **Scrape the flesh from the revealed leg bone.**

09 **Each thigh and drumstick will have part of the leg bone attached, giving it its French trim.**

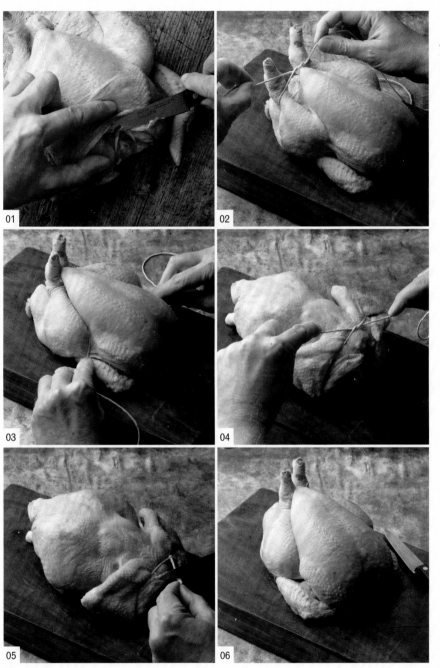

Trussing a bird ready for roasting

Trussing a bird before roasting it is not essential but it undoubtedly gives the bird a neater shape, which looks better when it is served at the table.

01 First remove the wishbone. Lay the bird on its back on a board. Pull back the flap of skin at the neck end and find the tip of the wishbone with a sharp small knife. Run the knife along the inside of the bone on both sides, then on the outside. Cut deeply enough to free the bone and make it clearly visible. Take care not to cut into the breast meat. Run the knife just behind the wishbone, then use your fingers to lift and twist it free.

02 Cut a piece of kitchen string about 4–5 times the length of the bird, then loop it around the narrowest part of each leg, pulling the ends tightly to bind the legs together.

03 Bring both ends of the string along either side of the breast, nestling it between the breast and the legs.

04 Take the string around the outside of the wings, flip the bird onto its breast and draw up the nub at the neck. Cross the ends of the string over the nub.

05 Holding the ends of the string and the nub, flip the bird onto its back again. Tie the ends of the string together into a tight knot at the nub of the neck.

06 Here you have the trussed bird, ready for the oven.

Stuffing a bird for roasting

See pp. 216–217 for my favourite recipes for stuffing your bird. My first tip when stuffing is, do not pack your bird too tightly, as the stuffing expands during cooking. Also, always stuff the bird just prior to cooking, never in advance, as this will increase the growth of bacteria. You can, by all means, make your stuffing in advance and refrigerate it, but only insert it just before roasting.

There are three methods of stuffing. The first, traditional, way is to place the stuffing inside the breast cavity (above). I am not completely convinced by this method, as it takes the bird longer to cook and, to avoid the risk of food poisoning, you must use a meat thermometer and make sure the bird reaches an internal temperature of 74°C (165°F).

The second method is to stuff the bird only at the neck end (above right). I prefer this but it reduces the quantity of stuffing you can use. After stuffing, ensure the neck flap is tucked under so the stuffing doesn't fall out during cooking, then finish by brushing the bird with oil.

The third method, and my preferred one, is to cook the stuffing separately. Place the prepared stuffing in a loaf tin lined with a sheet of baking parchment or aluminium foil. Cover the tin with foil and cook at 190°C (375°F/Gas 5) for 30 minutes, then remove the foil and cook for 30 minutes more for crisp stuffing.

Yet another option is to make stuffing balls. Roll the stuffing into walnut-sized balls, place in a shallow roasting tin lined with baking parchment, then drizzle with a little olive oil. Cook at 180°C (350°F/Gas 4 for 30 minutes until browned and crispy, shaking the tin occasionally to prevent the balls from sticking.

Stuffing under the skin

This method is used for preparations such as breasts, legs or spatchcocked birds. In these cases, you insert the stuffing under the skin or in a pocket cut into the meat (see p.54).

01 **Prepare your favourite flavoured butter (see p.210). Starting at the neck end of your bird, carefully ease your fingers under the breast skin (taking care not to split the skin as you go) to separate the skin from the flesh.**

02 **Push about half the flavoured butter under the skin, spreading it evenly all over the breast area.**

03 **Now smear the remainder of the butter liberally over the chicken, inside and out, and season with salt and pepper.**

04 **Transfer to a roasting dish. Adding a few herbs such as thyme or rosemary will give you the basis of a well-flavoured gravy.**

A GUIDE TO POULTRY ROASTING TIMES

Below is a guide to roasting times for whole unstuffed birds.
Add approximately 20 minutes more for a bird that is stuffed.

TYPE OF POULTRY	TIME / WEIGHT	ROASTING TEMPERATURE
Chicken	45 minutes per 1kg (2¼lb)	190°C (375°F/Gas 5) – 200°C (400°F/Gas 6)
Poussin	20 minutes per 450g (1lb)	190°C (375°F/Gas 5) – 200°C (400°F/Gas 6)
Turkey	45 minutes per 1kg (2¼lb), plus 20 minutes	190°C (375°F/Gas 5) – 200°C (400°F/Gas 6)
Goose	30 minutes per 1kg (2¼lb)	190°C (375°F/Gas 5) – 200°C (400°F/Gas 6)
Duck	45 minutes per 1kg (2¼lb)	180°C (350°F/Gas 4) – 190°C (375°F/Gas 5)
Guinea fowl	40 minutes per 1kg (2¼lb)	190°C (375°F/Gas 5) – 200°C (400°F/Gas 6)
Squab pigeon	15–20 minutes	190°C (375°F/Gas 5) – 200°C (400°F/Gas 6)
Quail	12–15 minutes	190°C (375°F/Gas 5) – 200°C (400°F/Gas 6)

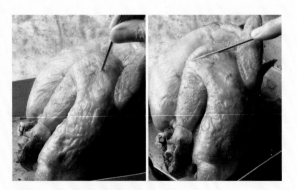

Checking a roasted bird for doneness

At the end of the roasting time, push a skewer or the point of a small knife into the thickest part of the thigh. If the juices that run out are clear, the bird is done; if they are pink, return the bird to the oven for 10 minutes more, then test again.

BASTING

Larger birds such as chicken, duck, guinea fowl and turkey are improved when basted regularly during roasting. This helps to keep the flesh moist. Baste with the drippings from the roasting tin or make a special baste (see p.215). Smaller birds such a quail or squab pigeon do not need to be basted.

RESTING POULTRY

Roasted poultry needs to be 'rested' before it is carved. This gives the cooking juices a chance to settle back into the meat, leaving it moist, juicy and easier to carve.

After cooking, place the bird on a plate and cover loosely with foil. Leave smaller birds such as chicken guinea fowl and duck to rest for 10–15 minutes, and larger birds for 25–30 minutes.

STOCK

Throughout this book you will occasionally need to use a stock to form the base of your sauce. Here are two simple chicken stocks – white stock and brown stock. They are simple to prepare, can be made in advance, and can be frozen if that suits you. Frozen stock will keep for up to three months. Thaw it slowly by leaving it in the fridge overnight.

White chicken stock

MAKES APPROX 2 LITRES (3½ PINTS/1.7 QUARTS)

1.5kg (3lb 3oz) chicken bones

3.5 litres (6 pints/2.2 quarts) water

1 leek, white part only, chopped

2 celery sticks, chopped

2 onions, chopped

1 garlic clove, unpeeled

2 sprigs of thyme

10 black peppercorns

Place the chicken bones in a large pan and add the water. Bring to the boil, skimming off any impurities that float to the surface.

Reduce the heat to its lowest, add the remaining ingredients and simmer for 3–4 hours.

Strain the stock through a muslin cloth (cheesecloth) or fine sieve (strainer) and leave to cool. If you are not using the stock immediately, you can refrigerate it for 3–4 days, or you can divide it into convenient quantities and freeze it.

Brown chicken stock

MAKES APPROX 3.5 LITRES (6 PINTS/2.2 QUARTS)

2kg (4½lb) chicken carcasses or wings, chopped

3 tbsp sunflower oil

2 carrots, chopped

2 celery sticks, chopped

2 garlic cloves, unpeeled

2 onions, chopped

2 tbsp tomato purée (paste)

2 sprigs of thyme

10 black peppercorns

4 litres (7 pints/3.4 quarts) water

Preheat the oven to 200°C (400°F/Gas 6).

Place the chicken in a roasting tin with the oil. Roast in the preheated oven for 45–60 minutes, stirring occasionally, until golden brown.

Remove from the oven and transfer the pieces of chicken to a large pan. Add the carrots, celery, garlic, onions, tomato purée (paste), thyme and peppercorns to the roasting tin and return the tin to the oven for 45 minutes, stirring occasionally until the vegetables are golden brown.

Transfer the vegetables to the pan with the chicken, then cover with the water.

Bring to the boil, skimming off any impurities that float to the surface. Reduce the heat to its lowest and simmer for 3–4 hours.

Strain the stock through a muslin cloth (cheesecloth) or fine sieve (strainer) and leave to cool. If you are not using the stock immediately, you can refrigerate it for 3–4 days or you can divide it into convenient quantities and freeze it.

ROASTING, PAN-ROASTING AND POT-ROASTING

Here I introduce you to your first three poultry cooking techniques. Roasting is simple but each type of bird has slightly different requirements, and you must allow some time for the bird to rest before carving it. Pan-roasting is used for cooking smaller joints of poultry. First you fry them in a pan to colour them and seal in the juices, then you transfer the joints to the oven to finish the cooking. To pot-roast, you sear the bird in a pan, then slow cook it, covered, and with minimum liquid. Finally, you remove the lid to allow the meat to colour.

Perfect roast chicken

I have yet to meet anyone who doesn't love a simply cooked, comforting roast chicken. Although many people are giving the traditional Sunday roast a miss, good old roast chicken seems to be undergoing a revival in many up-and-coming restaurants. I simply love the wonderful aromas given off as a roast chicken cooks, not to mention loving the look of anticipation on the faces around the table when it is about to be served. Everyone knows they are in for something special.

SERVES 4

1 x 1.5kg (3lb 3oz) chicken

4 sprigs of rosemary

2 sprigs of thyme

6 sage leaves

25g (scant 1oz/1¾ tbsp) unsalted butter, softened

2 tbsp sunflower oil

Sea salt and freshly ground black pepper

Preheat the oven to 190°C (375°F/Gas 5). Season the chicken well with salt and pepper. Place the rosemary, thyme and sage inside the body cavity.

Lift the breast skin from the neck end, insert your fingers between the skin and the flesh, and rub the breasts with your fingers to break the membranes connecting the skin to the breasts (see p.19, steps 1 and 2).

Carefully rub the breast all over with soft butter, taking care not to break the skin.

Heat the oil in a roasting tin over a medium heat. When it is hot, place the chicken in the tin and fry for 4–5 minutes until golden brown. Turn the chicken over and brown the other side.

Transfer the chicken to the preheated oven, breast upwards. Roast for 1 hour, or until the chicken is cooked and the juices run clear when the thigh is pierced with a skewer or small sharp knife. Baste the chicken with the cooking juices from time to time during cooking.

Remove the chicken from the oven and transfer to a plate. Cover with foil and leave to rest for 10 minutes before carving (see p.27).

Meanwhile, make a gravy from the roasting juices (see p.220).

Carve the chicken (see p.27) or cut it into joints (see p.26). Season with a little more salt before serving.

Slow-roasted chicken

Some people believe that cooking a chicken at the usual temperature of 190°C–200°C (375°F–400°F/Gas 5–6), as in the recipe above, makes the bird a little dry, since the protein strands in the bird contract, which forces the natural juices out. For cooks who are not in a rush, I suggest cooking the chicken the slow-roast way. After browning your bird in the roasting tin, cook it at 90°C (190°F/Gas ¼) for 4 hours. Try both methods, then decide which you prefer!

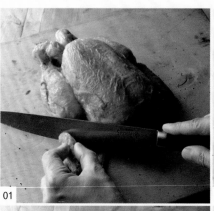

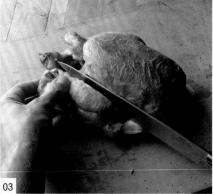

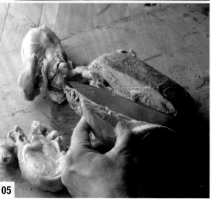

Jointing a cooked bird into 4
ABOVE

01 **Lay the bird breast side up on a board. Bend the wings outwards to locate the wing joints, then cut down firmly through the joints, severing the tendons.**

02 **Remove the winglets and the wings.**

03 **Cut between the thigh and the breast. Bend the thigh out to locate the hip joint.**

04 **Cut through the hip joint to remove the whole leg. Do the same on the other side.**

05 **French trim the breasts (see p.16), then remove these from the carcass.**

06 **You will now have four main pieces – two breast joints and two leg joints, plus two wings and two winglets.**

Jointing a cooked bird into 8
BELOW

01 **Cut the leg joints into two by cutting through the thigh bone to divide the thigh from the drumstick.**

02 **Cut the breast joints into two by cutting across on the diagonal.**

03 **You will now end up with eight main pieces, plus two wings and two winglets.**

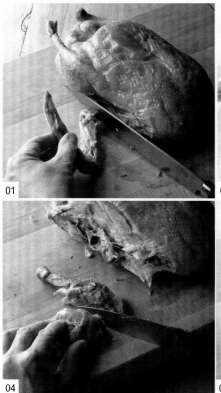

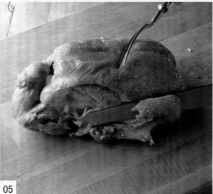

01
02
03
04
05
06

Carving a bird

01 **Lay the bird breast side up on a large board. Gently bend the wings to locate the wing joints, then cut down firmly through the joints, severing the tendons and separating the wings.**

02 **Cut between the thigh and the breast.**

03 **Bend the thigh outwards to locate the hip joint. Cut through the hip joint to remove the whole leg. Do the same on the other side.**

04 **Cut through the legs to divide each into a drumstick and a thigh.**

05 **Hold the bird steady with a carving fork. Using a long knife with a slender blade, start carving the breast, working from the outside towards the breastbone.**

06 **Carve the breast into neat, thin slices until you reach the breastbone.**

Whole roasted poussins *with lemon and herb purée*

Serving poussins is sure to impress your guests, and they cook faster than a chicken, too, so what's not to like? The lemon mixed with herbs and garlic that you use to rub under the skin and over the breasts really give this poussin dish a lift. The flavours are fresh and wonderfully vibrant.

SERVES 4

2 x 700–800g (1½–1¾lb) poussins

1 onion, finely chopped

25g (scant 1oz/1 cup) basil leaves

25g (scant 1oz/1 cup) flat-leaf parsley leaves

1 tbsp chopped rosemary

1 tbsp chopped mint leaves

Grated zest of 1 lemon

150ml (5fl oz/⅔ cup) olive oil

1 lemon, cut in half

1 head of garlic cut in half widthways

Sea salt and freshly ground black pepper

Preheat the oven to 200°C (400°F/Gas 6).

Rub the poussins inside and out with salt and pepper.

For the lemon and herb purée, place the onion, basil, parsley, rosemary, mint, lemon zest and a little salt and pepper in a blender. Blitz until finely chopped. With the machine still running, gradually add half the olive oil in a steady stream until you have a smooth, emulsified purée.

Stuff the poussins under the skin and over the breasts (see p.19) using the lemon and herb purée. Put one lemon half and one garlic half in each poussin cavity and drizzle over the remaining oil.

Place in a roasting tin in the preheated oven and roast for 15–20 minutes, basting from time to time with the roasting juices.

Reduce the oven temperature to 180°C (350°F/Gas 4) and return to the oven for 15 minutes more until the poussins are cooked and the juices run clear when the thigh is pierced with a skewer or small sharp knife.

Remove the poussins from the oven and transfer to a plate. Cover with foil and leave to rest for 10 minutes before carving (see p.27).

Truffled chicken breast forestière *with aligot*

Many home cooks regard fresh truffles as one of the ultimate luxury ingredients, far beyond their pockets. But you can find less expensive, good canned or bottled truffles in delis, and over the last two years, we have seen the emergence of the British truffle. These are excellent and well worth sourcing and, dare I say it, less costly than their French or Italian cousins.

SERVES 4

2 x 1.5kg (3lb 3oz) chickens, breast portions only (reserve the rest of the birds for another use)

1 medium truffle, cut into 10–12 very thin slices (ideally with a mandolin slicer)

4 tbsp sunflower oil

300g (11oz) mixed wild mushrooms, trimmed, washed and dried

1 shallot, finely chopped

2 tbsp chopped flat-leaf parsley

100ml (3½fl oz/scant ½ cup) Madeira wine

300ml (10fl oz/1¼ cups) brown chicken stock (see p.21)

25g (scant 1oz/1¾ tbsp) unsalted butter, chilled and cut into small cubes

Sea salt and freshly ground black pepper

FOR THE ALIGOT

800g (1¾lb) floury (mealy) potatoes (such as Desirée or Maris Piper), unpeeled

100g (3½oz/scant ½ cup) crème fraîche

75g (2½oz/5 tbsp) unsalted butter

½ garlic clove, crushed

200g (7oz) Tomme de Savoie cheese, rind removed and cut into small cubes

Lift the skin from the breasts, inserting your fingers between the skin and the flesh, and rubbing the breasts with your fingers to break the membranes connecting the skin to the breasts (see p.19, steps 1 and 2).

Carefully place 3 truffle slices on each breast, then fold the skin back on top. (If you prefer, you can do this a day in advance and keep the chicken breasts in the fridge, covered with clingfilm (plastic wrap).

Preheat the oven to 190°C (375°F/Gas 5).

Rub the chicken breasts with half the oil and season with salt and pepper. Put in a roasting tin in the preheated oven and roast for 45 minutes, or until the breasts are cooked and the juices run clear when pierced with a skewer or small sharp knife.

Meanwhile, make the aligot, put the potatoes in a pan with salt and cold water to cover. Bring to the boil, then reduce the heat and simmer until tender.

Drain the potatoes and when cool enough to handle, peel them and pass through a potato ricer.

In a pan, bring the crème fraîche, butter and garlic to the boil over a medium heat. Stir in the hot puréed potatoes. Working as quickly as possible, beat in the cheese a little at a time until the aligot is smooth, creamy and a little elastic. Season with salt and pepper. If necessary, remove from the heat and set aside, covered with a lid, to keep warm.

For the mushrooms, heat the remaining oil in a frying pan (skillet). When the oil is hot add the mushrooms, shallot and parsley. Season with salt and pepper and cook for 2–3 minutes, stirring occasionally.

When the chicken breasts are ready, remove from the oven and transfer to a plate. Cover with foil to keep warm while you make the sauce.

Pour off any excess fat from the roasting tin and put on the hob. Add the Madeira and stock and bring to the boil, stirring to loosen any caramelised bits from the bottom of the tin. Season, then strain through a fine sieve (strainer). Whisk in the chilled butter.

Carve the breasts (see p.27) and divide between the serving plates.

Spoon over the mushrooms and drizzle over the sauce. Serve with the aligot.

Stuffed poussin breasts
with aubergine caviar and tomato and basil sauce

Aubergine (eggplant) caviar is a delight. Here I use it to stuff poussin breasts, but it is wonderful with fish, lamb, beef, or just about anything. You can prepare it well in advance and keep it in the fridge until needed. Vine-ripened tomatoes are mouth-wateringly sweet. Here I use them to make a great tomato and basil sauce to complement my poussin breasts.

SERVES 4

2 aubergines (eggplants)

2 garlic cloves, thinly sliced

150ml (5fl oz/⅔ cup) olive oil

2 sprigs of thyme, leaves only

2 tsp smoked paprika (pimentón)

2 tbsp chopped pitted black olives

2 roasted red peppers (bell peppers) in oil, drained and finely chopped

1 tbsp chopped flat-leaf parsley

2 double poussins, approx 450–600g (1–1lb 5oz) each, breast portions only (reserve the rest of the birds for another use)

400g (14oz/2⅔ cups) cherry tomatoes on the vine

1 tsp caster (superfine) sugar

10 basil leaves, plus a few to garnish

2 courgettes (zucchini), cut into 1cm (½in) thick rounds

Sea salt and freshly ground black pepper

Preheat the oven to 170°C (325°F/Gas 3).

To make the aubergine (eggplant) caviar, cut the aubergines (eggplants) in half lengthways, then score the skin in a criss-cross fashion, taking care not to cut into the flesh. Place the aubergine (eggplant) halves, skin side up, on a large square of aluminium foil.

Put the slices of garlic in the score lines. Spoon over 100ml (3½fl oz/scant ½ cup) olive oil, sprinkle with the thyme and season with salt and a little pepper. Scrunch up the foil to form a pouch around the aubergine (eggplant) halves.

Transfer the pouch to a large baking tray (cookie sheet) and cook in the preheated oven for 45 minutes, or until the aubergine (eggplant) is tender. Remove from the oven, cool slightly, then carefully scrape the flesh from the skin using a spoon. Chop the flesh finely.

Put 1 tbsp oil in a frying pan (skillet) over a medium heat. When the oil is hot, add the chopped aubergine (eggplant) flesh and season with paprika. Add the olives and red peppers (bell peppers), and cook over a low heat for 5 minutes. Stir in the parsley and remove to a bowl. Leave to go cold.

Increase the oven temperature to 180°C (350°F/Gas 4).

When the aubergine (eggplant) caviar is cold, use it to stuff the poussin breasts under the skin (see p.19). Place the breasts in a roasting tin and drizzle over 1 tbsp oil. Season generously with salt and pepper and put in the preheated oven.

Meanwhile, prepare the tomato sauce. Put 100g (3½oz/⅔ cup) cherry tomatoes in a small pan with 1 tbsp oil and the sugar and basil. Cook over a low heat for 5–8 minutes, or until the tomatoes become soft and break up. Place in a blender or use a stick blender to blitz to a smooth purée. Strain through a coarse sieve (strainer) into a clean pan. Set aside.

When the breasts have been in the oven for 15 minutes, add the courgettes (zucchini) to the tin and toss with the cooking juices. Return to the oven. After 5 more minutes, add the remaining cherry tomatoes and cook for 10–12 minutes more until the breasts are golden and cooked, and the juices run clear when they are pierced with a skewer or small sharp knife. Remove from the oven and leave to rest for 5 minutes.

Gently reheat the tomato sauce.

Divide the breasts between the serving plates. Put the roasted courgettes (zucchini) and tomatoes alongside. Drizzle the hot tomato sauce around the chicken, garnish with basil leaves and serve immediately.

Spatchcocked poussins *with herby ricotta stuffing*

Once you have spatchcocked and marinated your poussins, it is easy to prepare this stuffing and slip it under the skin. Not only does it taste delicious but it also protects the flesh from the heat of the oven or griddle, keeping it moist and truly succulent. Use a firm ricotta, ideally from an Italian deli. If you are using ricotta from a tub, drain it in a sieve (strainer) set over a bowl overnight before use.

SERVES 4

4 poussins, spatchcocked (see below)

1 quantity Simple Olive Oil, Garlic and Lemon Marinade (see p.212)

200g (7oz/scant 1 cup) firm ricotta cheese

1 garlic clove, crushed

50g (1¾oz/1⅔ cups) mixed herbs (tarragon, flat-leaf parsley, oregano), roughly chopped

25g (scant 1oz/scant ¼ cup) grated Parmesan cheese

Grated zest of ½ lemon

1 egg, beaten

100g (3½oz/generous 1¾ cups) fresh white breadcrumbs

2 tbsp olive oil

Sea salt and freshly ground black pepper

The day before, place the poussins in a large dish with the Simple Olive Oil, Garlic and Lemon Marinade. Cover with clingfilm (plastic wrap) and put in the fridge to marinate overnight.

The next day, make the stuffing. Put the ricotta in a bowl and add the garlic, herbs, Parmesan, lemon zest, egg, and salt and pepper. Stir in the breadcrumbs and mix well.

Remove the poussins from the marinade and stuff them under the skin and over the breasts and legs (see p.19) using the ricotta stuffing.

Preheat the oven to 180°C (350°F/Gas 4).

Put the poussins in a roasting tin and drizzle over the olive oil. Put in the preheated oven and roast for about 25 minutes, or until the poussins are cooked and the juices run clear when the thighs are pierced with a skewer or small sharp knife.

Spatchcocking

Lay the bird breast side up on a board. Using poultry shears or kitchen scissors, cut either side of the backbone to cut the backbone away.

Turn the chicken so it is breast side up and flatten it slightly. Use the heel of your hand to press firmly along the breastbone. The breastbone and the wishbone will break and the bird will lie flat.

Right: The spatchcocked poussins in their marinade.

Roast quail *with pumpkin and chestnuts, and mustard quinoa*

Allow two quails per person for this dish and do not overcook them. They are best served slightly pink or they can be a little on the dry side. If you like, you could use poussins instead of quail. Serving the quail with quinoa, the easy-to-cook South American super-grain, turns this dish into a wholesome meal.

SERVES 4

2 tbsp sunflower oil

50g (1¾oz) smoked bacon lardons

350g (12oz/3 cups) pumpkin, skin removed, cut into 1cm (½in) cubes

200g (7oz) chestnuts (frozen or vacuum-packed)

30g (1oz/2 tbsp) unsalted butter

8 quails

75ml (2½fl oz/⅓ cup) cider vinegar or white wine vinegar

125ml (4½fl oz/½ cup) dry white wine

600ml (1 pint/2½ cups) brown chicken stock (see p.21)

12 tarragon leaves, chopped

Sea salt and freshly ground black pepper

FOR THE QUINOA

1 tbsp sunflower oil

25g (scant 1oz/1¾ tbsp) unsalted butter

200g (7oz/generous 1 cup) quinoa

600ml (1 pint/2½ cups) boiling water

2 tsp wholegrain mustard

Preheat the oven to 200°C (400°F/Gas 6).

Heat 2 tbsp oil in a roasting tin over a medium heat. When the oil is hot, add the lardons and fry for about 5 minutes until golden and crispy.

Add the pumpkin and chestnuts and toss with the lardons. Transfer to the preheated oven for 15–20 minutes until the pumpkin and chestnuts have caramelised. Season with salt and pepper.

Meanwhile, prepare the quinoa. Heat the oil and butter in a pan, and when they are hot, add the quinoa. Stirring continuously, cook over a low-medium heat until the quinoa gives off a nutty fragrance.

Add the boiling water, stir well, then simmer for 12–15 minutes, or until the water has been absorbed and the grains are light and fluffy. Season with salt and pepper, then stir in the mustard. If necessary, set aside, covered with a lid, to keep warm.

Meanwhile, cook the quails. Heat the remaining oil and 10g (¼oz/¾ tbsp) butter in a roasting tin over a medium heat. When they are hot, add the quails and fry for 2–3 minutes until brown all over. Season with salt and pepper. Add the pumpkin and chestnuts to the tin and transfer to the oven.

Roast for 12–15 minutes. Remove from the oven and leave to rest for 5 minutes.

Divide the quail into breast and leg portions and transfer to a plate. Cover with foil to keep warm while you prepare the tarragon sauce.

Transfer the quail carcasses to a small pan and add the vinegar and wine. Bring to the boil, then reduce the heat and simmer for 2–3 minutes. Add the stock, bring back to the boil, then reduce the heat again and simmer until the liquid has reduced by half.

Strain the sauce though a fine sieve (strainer) into a clean pan. Whisk in the remaining butter and add the tarragon.

Divide the quail breasts and legs between the serving plates. Add the pumpkin and chestnuts and a generous helping of mustard quinoa. Pour the tarragon sauce over the quails and serve immediately.

Barbecued roast duck breasts Peking style

Traditionally prepared Peking duck is made by air-drying the duck, then cooking it whole, and finally glazing it in the oven in an aromatic, sweet, sticky glaze. This is a long process. My recipe uses duck breasts and involves a lot less fuss. I serve mine with a sweet onion jam and I often also accompany it with some chilli-roasted king oyster mushrooms and sweet potatoes.

SERVES 4

2 tbsp olive oil

2 orange sweet potatoes, cut into 1cm (½in) cubes

½ tsp chopped red chilli

300g (11oz) king oyster mushrooms

4 x 180g (scant 6½oz) duck breasts, skin on and excess fat removed

Sea salt and freshly ground black pepper

FOR THE GLAZE

2cm (¾in) piece of root ginger, peeled and grated

4 tbsp hoisin sauce

1 tsp Chinese five-spice powder

2 tbsp clear honey

2 tbsp mirin (sweet rice wine) or dry sherry

1 garlic clove, crushed

FOR THE ONION JAM

2 tbsp olive oil

2 tbsp caster (superfine) sugar

2 large onions, thinly sliced

2cm (¾in) piece of root ginger, peeled and finely chopped

3 tbsp rice wine vinegar or white wine vinegar

2 tbsp chopped coriander (cilantro)

Preheat the oven to 150°C (300°F/Gas 2).

Heat the oil in a small roasting tin. Add the sweet potatoes and chilli, and season with salt and pepper. Roast in the preheated oven for 20 minutes, then add the mushrooms. Roast for 10 minutes more until the vegetables are cooked and golden.

Meanwhile, bring a pan of water to the boil, immerse the duck breasts in the water and cook over a low heat for 3 minutes to blanch them. Remove from the water, leave to cool, then dry on a clean tea towel (dishtowel). Set aside.

For the glaze, place the ginger, hoisin sauce, Chinese five-spice powder, honey, mirin and garlic in a small pan over a medium heat. Cook for 5 minutes, stirring occasionally.

Brush the duck breasts liberally with the glaze, then put in a clean roasting tin.

Roast in the oven for 10–15 minutes, alongside the sweet potatoes and mushrooms, until the duck breasts are caramelised.

Meanwhile, prepare the onion jam. Put the oil in a heavy-based pan over a medium heat. When the oil is hot, add the sugar and onions and cook for 8–10 minutes until the onions are lightly golden. Add the ginger and vinegar and cook for 5 minutes more. Stir in the coriander (cilantro) and season with salt and pepper. Set aside, if necessary, covered with a lid to keep warm.

Remove the roasted duck breasts from the tin and reserve the cooking juices.

Cut the breasts in half or into thick slices. To serve, divide the roasted sweet potatoes and mushrooms between the serving plates and top each with some duck breast. Place the onion jam alongside and pour over the cooking juices.

Roast duck *with lavender honey, turnips, parsnips and raisins*

You may have a few reservations about cooking a dish using duck with lavender, but this recipe will soon convert you. The resulting sauce has a wonderful rich flavour and the sweet-and-sour caramelised root vegetables help balance the dish to perfection.

SERVES 4

4 tbsp lavender flowers (fresh or dried)

1 tbsp thyme leaves

½ tsp cracked black peppercorns

1 tsp coarse sea salt

1 x 2kg (4½lb) whole duck

100ml (3½fl oz/scant ½ cup) good-quality red wine vinegar

800ml (28fl oz/3½ cups) brown chicken stock (see p.21)

2 tbsp lavender honey or clear honey

FOR THE VEGETABLES

25g (scant 1oz/1¾ tbsp) unsalted butter

4 parsnips, cut into 4 lengthways

400g (14oz) baby turnips, trimmed

1 tbsp light brown sugar

2 tbsp red wine vinegar

500ml (16fl oz/generous 2 cups) brown chicken stock (see p.21)

50g (1¾oz/scant ⅔ cup) raisins, soaked in warm water for 30 minutes, then drained

Preheat the oven to 200°C (400°F/Gas 6).

Place the lavender flowers in a mortar with the thyme, peppercorns and sea salt. Grind to a powder.

With a knife, lightly score the duck breasts in a criss-cross pattern, taking care not to cut right through. Rub the duck liberally with half the lavender mixture.

Place the duck in a roasting tin and roast in the preheated oven for about 1¾ hours until cooked.

Remove from the oven, transfer to a plate and set aside.

Pour off any excess fat from the roasting tin and place the tin over a medium heat. Add the vinegar and stock and bring to the boil.

Return the duck to the roasting tin. Spoon over the stock mixture and brush with half the honey.

Return the duck to the oven and cook for about 15 minutes until caramelised. While the duck is cooking, baste it once or twice with the pan juices, brush it with the remaining half of the honey and sprinkle over the remaining lavender mixture.

While the duck is in the oven for its final cooking, prepare the vegetables.

Heat the butter in a large lidded frying pan (skillet). When the butter is hot, add the parsnips and turnips. Sauté for 4–5 minutes, or until they begin to colour.

Sprinkle over the brown sugar and toss together for 1 minute. Add the vinegar.

Add the stock and raisins and cover with a lid. Bring to the boil then reduce the heat and simmer for 10–12 minutes until the vegetables are just tender and beautifully caramelised. Remove from the heat and keep warm, covered with the lid.

When the duck is ready, remove it from the oven. Strain the cooking juices from the roasting tin into a small pan.

Cut the duck into 8 pieces. Pour the cooking juices over and serve with the caramelised vegetables.

Roast guinea fowl *with wild garlic pesto stuffing*

I always look forward to spring time. With the new crops of vegetables and herbs coming into season, it is one of my favourite times of year for cooking. The wild garlic that arrives along with spring is a special favourite of mine. It only makes a brief appearance but when it does, I use it as often as possible.

SERVES 4

2 x 600–700g (1lb 5oz–1½lb) guinea fowl

4 tbsp olive oil

15g (½oz/1 tbsp) unsalted butter

1 carrot, finely chopped

1 onion, finely chopped

1 celery stick, finely chopped

400ml (14fl oz/1¾ cups) brown chicken stock (see p.21)

1 small bay leaf

Sprig of rosemary

Sea salt and freshly ground black pepper

FOR THE PESTO STUFFING

Good handful of wild garlic leaves

2 garlic cloves, crushed

75g (2½oz/½ cup) pine nuts, toasted

40g (scant 1½oz) Parmesan cheese

1 egg yolk

100g (3½oz/generous 1¾ cups) fine fresh white breadcrumbs

Start by making the pesto stuffing. Place the wild garlic leaves, garlic, pine nuts and Parmesan in a food processor. Blitz to a coarse purée, then transfer to a bowl. Stir in the egg yolk and breadcrumbs. Season with salt and pepper and set aside.

Preheat the oven to 190°C (375°F/Gas 5).

Remove the wings from the guinea fowl. Season the cavity of each bird and season liberally all over.

Stuff the cavities of the birds (see p.18) with the pesto stuffing and secure the openings by tying the legs together with kitchen string. Alternatively, you can stuff the neck end of the birds or cook the stuffing separately.

Put 2 tbsp oil and the butter in a roasting tin over a medium heat. When the fats are hot, add the guinea fowl, breast side down, and fry each side of the breast for 2–3 minutes until golden. Transfer the birds to the preheated oven and cook for 15 minutes.

Reduce the temperature of the oven to 170°C (325°F/Gas 3).

Cover the guinea fowl with foil and return to the oven for 40–45 minutes more, or until they are cooked and the juices run clear when the thigh is pierced with a skewer or small sharp knife.

Meanwhile, make the sauce. Put the remaining oil in a medium pan over a medium heat. When the oil is hot, add the guinea fowl wings and fry for 8–10 minutes until golden. Add the carrot, onion and celery and fry for 5 minutes more.

Pour over the chicken stock and bring to the boil. Add the bay leaf and rosemary, reduce the heat and simmer for 25 minutes. Strain through a fine sieve (strainer) into a small pan. Season with salt and pepper and set aside.

When the guinea fowl are ready, remove from the oven and transfer to a plate. Cover with foil and leave to rest for 10 minutes before carving (see p.27).

Meanwhile, pour off any excess fat from the roasting tin and place the tin over a medium heat. Add the prepared sauce, bring to the boil and boil for 2 minutes.

Divide the pesto stuffing between the serving plates and place the guinea fowl on top. Pour over the sauce and serve immediately.

Roast goose *with fennel and celery, and quince compote*

People often think that goose is a tricky bird to cook. It's regarded as extremely fatty and best consigned to the Christmas table. It's true that it does produce a fair amount of fat as it cooks but that isn't a disadvantage as far as I'm concerned and I think goose deserves to be used more often. Once you've learned how to cook it, you'll soon enjoy its rich, tasty meat. Offset that richness with a fruit compote. Here I use quince, but apple or pear would be fantastic, too.

Remember, however big your goose, it doesn't provide nearly as much meat as you might expect. But it will always be delicious!

SERVES 6	3 tbsp maple syrup or clear honey	**FOR THE QUINCE COMPOTE**
1 x 4.5–6kg (9–12lb) goose	3 tbsp red wine vinegar	**2 large quinces**
8 celery sticks	Good pinch of ground star anise	**200g (7oz/1 cup) caster (superfine) sugar**
2 heads of fennel	Sea salt and freshly ground black pepper	**250ml (8fl oz/1 cup) water**
2 sprigs of rosemary chopped	Watercress, to garnish	**2 tsp chopped rosemary**
2 sprigs of thyme, chopped		

Preheat the oven to 180°C (350°F/Gas 4). Prick the skin to allow the fat to drain (see below). Season the cavity of the goose liberally with salt and pepper. Rub more salt into the skin. Put the goose on a roasting rack set above a large roasting tin.

Put in the preheated oven and roast for 2 hours. You do not need to baste during cooking as the goose produces plenty of fat and is effectively self-basting.

While the goose is in the oven, peel the celery and fennel. Cut the fennel into wedges and the celery into 7.5cm (3in) lengths.

After 2 hours, briefly remove the goose to a plate and drain off all but 2 tbsp of the fat.

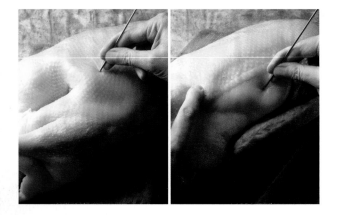

Add the celery and fennel to the roasting tin. Toss with the fat, then add the rosemary and thyme. Return the goose to the tin on top of the celery and fennel. Roast for 30 minutes more.

While the goose is cooking, make the quince compote. Peel, core and cut the quinces into 2cm (¾in) cubes. Place in a pan with the sugar and water over a medium heat. Cover and cook for 45 minutes, or until the quinces are soft. Add the chopped rosemary and set aside. (You can add more sugar or rosemary according to taste.)

After 30 minutes cooking, remove the goose from the oven.

Mix the maple syrup, vinegar and star anise together in a bowl and brush the mixture liberally over the goose. Return the goose to the oven for a final 15 minutes. When the goose is cooked, it should feel slightly springy to the touch and the juices should run slightly pink but almost clear.

Remove the goose from the oven and leave to rest for 15 minutes before carving (see p.27). Transfer the celery and fennel to a small pan. When ready to serve, quickly reheat the celery and fennel. Garnish the goose with watercress and serve with the roast celery and fennel, and with the quince compote alongside.

Roast quail

with creamy horseradish cabbage, smoked bacon and chestnuts

This dish is the perfect winter-time treat – creamy Savoy cabbage enhanced with horseradish, plus smoky roast bacon, potatoes and chestnuts.

SERVES 4

350g (12oz) new baby potatoes, unpeeled

150g (5½oz) smoked bacon lardons

200g (7oz) chestnuts (frozen or vacuum-packed)

40g (scant 1½oz/3 tbsp) unsalted butter, plus 1 tbsp for reheating the cabbage leaves

4 large quails, approx 550g (1¼lb) each

4 tbsp sunflower oil

1 small Savoy cabbage, blemished outer leaves removed

100ml (3½fl oz/scant ½ cup) double (heavy) cream

2 tbsp creamed horseradish

100ml (3½fl oz/scant ½ cup) Madeira

300ml (10fl oz/1¼ cups) brown chicken stock (see p.21)

Sea salt and freshly ground black pepper

Preheat the oven to 200°C (400°F/Gas 6).

Put the potatoes and lardons in a roasting tin and season with salt and pepper.

Roast for 20 minutes in the preheated oven, then add the chestnuts and 25g (scant 1oz/1¾ tbsp) butter. Toss together and return to the oven to cook for 15 minutes more, until golden and cooked through.

Meanwhile, place the quails in another roasting tin. Season with salt and pepper and drizzle with 2 tbsp oil. Roast for 12–15 minutes in the oven together with the potatoes, bacon and chestnuts.

Meanwhile, prepare the horseradish cabbage. Remove 8 whole outer leaves from the cabbage and blanch in boiling water for 5 minutes. Leaving the hot water in the pan, remove the cabbage leaves with a slotted spoon, drain well and set aside.

Shred the remaining cabbage and add to the water in the pan. Cook for 2 minutes then drain well.

Put 1 tbsp butter in a small pan over a medium heat. When the butter is hot, add the blanched shredded cabbage, the cream and the horseradish. Cook for 5 minutes, or until the cream has reduced and the cabbage is bound in a thick sauce. Remove from the heat and cover with a lid to keep warm.

When the quails are cooked, remove from the oven and leave to rest for 5 minutes. Carve each quail into breast and leg portions (see p.26) and keep warm, covered with foil.

Meanwhile, make the sauce. Place the quail bones and Madeira in a pan, add the stock and bring to the boil. Boil for 5 minutes until the sauce has thickened and reduced by half. Strain through a fine sieve (strainer) and season with salt and pepper. Set aside, covered with foil, to keep warm.

To reheat the cabbage leaves, put 1 tbsp butter in a pan over a medium heat. When the butter is hot, add the cabbage leaves and toss quickly in the butter.

To serve, arrange 2 cabbage leaves in the centre of each serving plate and top with some of the creamy horseradish cabbage.

Place the smoky roast bacon, potatoes and chestnut garnish around the cabbage, then top with the quail portions. Pour over the sauce and serve immediately.

Stuffed roasted turkey breast *with persian dried fruits and hazelnuts*

Turkey is a great low-fat alternative to meat that, in my opinion, deserves to be eaten more often. When cooked with care, it can be delicious, juicy and moist. The Persian stuffing I suggest here is wonderfully fruity and goes really well with other poultry, too, such as guinea fowl, chicken or duck.

SERVES 6–8

1 x 3kg (6½lb) turkey breast

3 tbsp sunflower oil

Sea salt and freshly ground black pepper

Watercress salad, to serve

FOR THE STUFFING

100g (3½oz/7 tbsp) unsalted butter

2 onions, finely chopped

1 tsp ground cumin

½ tsp ground turmeric

150g (5½oz/generous 1 cup) dried prunes, soaked in warm water for 30 minutes, then drained

120g (scant 4½oz/⅔ cup) dried apricots, soaked in warm water for 30 minutes, then drained

50g (1¾oz/scant ⅔ cup) raisins

1 tsp ground cinnamon

75g (2½oz/½ cup) skinned hazelnuts, toasted and chopped

4 slices white bread, cut into small cubes

Grated zest of ½ lemon

First make the stuffing. Put the butter in a frying pan (skillet) over a medium heat. When the butter is hot, add the onions, cumin and turmeric. Cook for 4–5 minutes, or until the onions are softened.

Coarsely chop the prunes and apricots and add to the pan with the raisins. Cook for 3 minutes more.

Transfer the mixture to a bowl and add the cinnamon, hazelnuts, bread and lemon zest. Season well with salt and pepper, and leave to cool.

Preheat the oven to 190°C (375°F/Gas 5).

Cut a lengthways slit in the turkey breast, about two-thirds of the way across, to form a pocket. Take care not cut right through (below left). Open up the breast and season with salt and pepper.

Place the stuffing in the slit (below centre), then close the pocket and tie the breast at intervals with kitchen string (below right).

Heat the oil in a large roasting tin over a medium heat. When the oil is hot, add the stuffed breast and fry all over until golden to seal it.

Place the turkey in the preheated oven, cover with foil and cook for 50–60 minutes, or until the juices run clear when the meat is pierced with a skewer or small sharp knife. Take care not to overcook the stuffed breast or the meat will become dry.

Serve with the pan gravy and a simple watercress salad.

Breast of chicken saltimbocca *with chestnut polenta*

The literal translation of *saltimbocca* is 'jump in the mouth' – an apt description of how the combination of simple flavours come to life in one dish. Traditionally, it is made with thin escalopes (scallops) of veal, but chicken works just as well and is far less expensive.

SERVES 4

4 x 160g (5½oz) French-trim chicken breasts (see p.16), skin on

4 slices of buffalo mozzarella

4 slices of Parma ham or prosciutto

2 tbsp olive oil

6 small sage leaves

100ml (3½fl oz/scant ½ cup) dry white wine

150ml (5fl oz/⅔ cup) brown chicken stock (see p.21)

15g (½oz/1 tbsp) unsalted butter, chilled

Sea salt and freshly ground black pepper

FOR THE POLENTA

75ml (2½fl oz/⅓ cup) double (heavy) cream

75g (2½oz) unsweetened chestnut purée

1 litre (1¾ pints/4 cups) water

150ml (5fl oz/⅔ cup) full-fat (whole) milk

150g (5½oz/1¼ cups) quick-cook polenta (cornmeal)

100g (3½oz/7 tbsp) unsalted butter, chilled and cut into small pieces

50g (1¾oz) Parmesan cheese

Freshly grated nutmeg

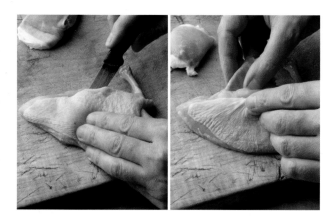

Make a 7.5cm (3in) deep cut with a small knife in the side of each chicken breast to form a pocket (above left).

Wrap each slice of mozzarella in a slice of Parma ham, then carefully stuff the wrapped mozzarella in the pocket in each chicken breast (above right).

Preheat the oven to 200°C (400°F/Gas 6).

Put the oil in a shallow ovenproof frying pan (skillet) over a medium heat. When the oil is hot, add the chicken breasts, skin side down, together with 3 sage leaves. Fry for 3–4 minutes until the sage has crispened up. Carefully turn the breasts over, then transfer the frying pan (skillet) to the preheated oven and cook for 12–15 minutes more.

Meanwhile, prepare the polenta (cornmeal). Put the cream and chestnut purée in a pan and slowly bring to the boil, whisking all the time.

Add the water and milk, reduce the heat to a simmer, then gradually rain in the polenta (cornmeal), stirring all the time to prevent it forming clumps. Cook, uncovered, for 10–15 minutes, stirring frequently until the mixture is smooth and thick. Beat in the butter and Parmesan. Season to taste with salt, pepper and a little freshly grated nutmeg. Cover the pan with a lid to keep warm.

When the chicken breasts are cooked, remove from the oven and transfer to a plate. Cover with foil to keep warm.

Meanwhile, prepare the sauce. Return the pan in which the chicken was cooked to the hob and pour off any excess fat. Add the wine, bring to the boil and boil for 1 minute. Add the stock and the remaining sage leaves. Bring back to the boil and boil until the sauce has reduced by half. Whisk in the chilled butter and season with salt and pepper.

To serve, divide the chestnut polenta between the serving plates, top with the chicken breasts and pour over the sauce.

Pan-roasted guinea fowl
with smoked bacon, vegetables and mustard sauce

Wrapping the guinea fowl breasts in rashers (slices) of bacon helps keep the flesh moist and juicy. As the bird cooks, the bacon releases its tasty fat.

SERVES 4

4 x 175g (6oz) French-trim guinea fowl breasts (see p.16), skin removed

1 tbsp chopped rosemary

4 tbsp sunflower oil

2 tsp Dijon mustard

8 thin rashers (slices) of smoked bacon

1 small celeriac

200g (7oz) baby carrots, trimmed

200g (7oz) baby parsnips

150g (5½oz) Italian cipollini onions, halved

50g (1¾oz/3½ tbsp) unsalted butter

650ml (23fl oz/generous 2¾ cups) brown chicken stock (see p.21)

Sea salt and freshly ground black pepper

Place the guinea fowl breasts in a shallow dish. Sprinkle over half the rosemary, 2 tbsp oil and 1 tsp Dijon mustard. Leave to marinate at room temperature for 1 hour.

Remove the breasts from the marinade and wrap each one in 2 rashers (slices) of bacon. Secure with a cocktail stick (toothpick) and season with salt and pepper.

Preheat the oven to 200°C (400°F/Gas 6).

Heat the remaining oil in an ovenproof frying pan (skillet) over a medium heat. When the oil is hot, add the breasts and cook for 3–4 minutes on each side until coloured.

Meanwhile, peel the celeriac and cut into 1cm (½in) cubes. Add the carrots, parsnips, onions, celeriac and butter to the pan and fry until the vegetables are golden.

Transfer the pan to the preheated oven and cook for 18–20 minutes until the guinea fowl breasts and the vegetables are tender and golden.

Remove from the oven and transfer the breasts and vegetables to a dish. Remove the cocktail sticks (toothpicks) and cover with foil to keep warm while you prepare the sauce.

Drain off any excess fat from the pan and add the remaining rosemary and the stock. Bring to the boil and boil for 5 minutes until the roasting juices have reduced and are thick enough to coat the back of a spoon. Whisk in the remaining Dijon mustard, then strain through a fine sieve (strainer).

Divide the guinea fowl breasts and the vegetables between the serving plates, pour over the sauce and serve immediately.

Smoke and salt-roasted duck
with confit leeks and broad beans, and white onion purée

I really love the different varieties of sea salts that are available nowadays. Smoked sea salt is one of my favourites; here I use it combined with regular sea salt to create lightly salted duck breasts that end up having just a hint of smokiness.

SERVES 4

4 x 180g (scant 6½oz) duck breasts, skin on, excess fat removed

FOR SALTING

175g (6oz/½ cup) sea salt

1 tbsp Maldon smoked sea salt

1 egg white

1 tbsp thyme leaves

1 garlic clove, crushed

2–3 bay leaves

FOR THE ONION PURÉE

2 tbsp olive oil

Sprig of thyme

2 large onions, chopped

100ml (3½fl oz/scant ½ cup) water

200ml (7fl oz/scant 1 cup) double (heavy) cream

3 tbsp full-fat (whole) milk

FOR THE LEEK AND BROAD (FAVA) BEAN CONFIT

75ml (2½fl oz/⅔ cup) water

50g (1¾oz/3½ tbsp) unsalted butter

12 baby leeks

300g (11oz) broad (fava) beans, podded weight

The day before, salt the duck breasts. Put both types of salt in a bowl and add the egg white, thyme, garlic and bay leaves. Use this marinade liberally, sprinkling it all over the breasts. Place the breasts in a large dish and sprinkle over any remaining salt mix. Cover with clingfilm (plastic wrap) and refrigerate overnight.

The next day, remove the breasts from the fridge and wipe off all the salt using kitchen paper (paper towels).

Bring a large pan of water to the boil, add the duck breasts and blanch for 2 minutes. Remove from the water, leave to cool, then dry on a clean tea towel (dishtowel).

Preheat the oven to 120°C (250°F/Gas ½).

Heat a large ovenproof frying pan (skillet) over a medium heat. When the pan is hot, add the duck breasts, skin side down, and fry for 3–4 minutes on each side until golden.

Transfer the pan with the breasts to the preheated oven for 30–40 minutes until the breasts are cooked and springy to the touch.

While the duck is in the oven, prepare the onion purée. (If you prefer, you can make this the day before.) Put the oil in a pan over a medium heat.

When the oil is hot, add the thyme and fry for 1 minute. Add the onions and water. Cover with a lid and cook for about 5 minutes until the onions are soft.

Add the cream and milk and bring to the boil.

Reduce the heat and simmer until the onions are tender and the liquid has nearly all evaporated. Remove the thyme. Transfer the mixture to a blender and blitz to a smooth purée. Season with salt and pepper and place in a clean pan. Set aside.

When the duck breasts are ready, remove from the oven and leave to rest for 5–8 minutes.

Meanwhile, prepare the leek and broad (fava) bean confit. Put the water and butter in a small pan and bring to the boil. Boil for a few minutes to form a light emulsion. Add the leeks and broad (fava) beans. Bring to the boil then reduce the heat and simmer gently for 8–10 minutes until the vegetables are tender. Drain, then season with salt and pepper.

Quickly reheat the onion purée and divide it between the serving plates. Cut the duck breasts into thin slices and divide between the serving plates. Spoon over the leek and broad (fava) bean confit and serve immediately.

Squab pigeon
with cherries, beetroot and granola, and parsnip-chocolate purée

When cherries are in season, they make a wonderful accompaniment to all sorts of poultry and game, such as duck, venison and squab pigeon. In this recipe, a little sprinkling of granola adds a pleasant crunch and makes a great contrast to the parsnip-chocolate purée.

SERVES 4

2 tbsp sunflower oil

4 x 450g (1lb) squab pigeons

200ml (7fl oz/scant 1 cup) good-quality red wine

100ml (3½fl oz/scant ½ cup) port

2 tbsp clear honey

400ml (14fl oz/1¾ cups) brown chicken stock (see p.21)

350g (12oz/2¼ cups) fresh red cherries, stoned, or frozen cherries

1 tbsp kirsch (optional)

Sea salt and freshly ground black pepper

50g (1¾oz/ scant ½ cup) granola, to serve

FOR THE PURÉE

500g (1lb 2oz) large crisp parsnips, chopped

100g (3½oz) potatoes, chopped

200ml (7fl oz/scant 1 cup) full-fat (whole) milk

600ml (1 pint/2½ cups) water

50g (1¾oz/3½ tbsp) unsalted butter

3 tbsp double (heavy) cream

75g (2½oz) white chocolate, melted in a bain-marie

FOR THE PICKLED BEETROOT

2 small raw beetroots, well washed

1 tbsp clear honey

1 tbsp balsamic vinegar

It is best to make the parsnip-chocolate purée (but do not add the chocolate) and the pickled beetroot the day before. For the purée, put the parsnips, potatoes, milk and water in a large pan. Bring to the boil, then reduce the heat and simmer for 25 minutes until the vegetables are soft. Drain well and pass through a potato ricer.

Return the purée to a clean pan, add the butter and cream, and mix well. Refrigerate overnight.

For the pickled beetroot, place the beetroots in a pan, cover with water and bring to the boil. Reduce the heat and simmer for about 1 hour, depending on their size, until tender. The beetroots are ready when they offer no resistance when pierced with a small knife. Remove and cool slightly, then peel.

Slice thinly using a mandolin slicer. Place in a bowl, add the honey and vinegar and mix well together. Refrigerate overnight.

The next day, preheat the oven to 200°C (400°F/Gas 6). Place the oil in a large ovenproof frying pan (skillet) over a medium heat. When the oil is hot, add the squab pigeons, breast side down, and fry for about 5 minutes on each side of the breast until coloured.

Turn the squab pigeons breast side up, and transfer the pan to the preheated oven. Roast for 8 minutes, then remove and transfer to a plate. Cover with foil and leave to rest for 5 minutes while you prepare the sauce and finish the purée.

For the sauce, drain off the excess fat from the roasting tin. Add the red wine and port, bring to the boil and boil for 2 minutes. Add the honey, chicken stock and cherries. Simmer until the sauce has reduced by a third. Add the kirsch, if using, and season with salt and pepper.

Reheat the purée over a low heat until it is hot, then stir in the melted white chocolate. Stir until smooth and creamy. Season with salt and pepper.

Joint the squab pigeons into breast and leg portions (see p.26). Place some pickled beetroot in the centre of a plate and top with the squab pigeon. Pour over the cherry sauce and sprinkle over the granola. Serve with the parsnip-chocolate purée alongside.

Pot-roasted chicken
with bay, prunes, bacon and onions, and bread sauce

The charms of this dish are not only its taste but also the fact that it uses minimal equipment. That's a real bonus for any cook. Combining bacon and prunes in cooking is something that goes back to the sixteenth century. The result is a lovely balance of salty and sweet flavours.

SERVES 4

2 tbsp olive oil

250g (9oz) piece of pancetta, cut into lardons

300g (11oz) button onions, peeled

200g (7oz) small shallots

2 tbsp caster (superfine) sugar

180g (scant 6½oz/1⅓ cups) prunes, pitted

600ml (1 pint/2½ cups) brown chicken stock (see p.21)

100ml (3½fl oz/scant ½ cup) dry white wine

1 x 1.5–2kg (3lb 3oz–4½lb) chicken

8 small bay leaves

25g (scant 1oz/1¾ tbsp) unsalted butter, melted

Sea salt and freshly ground black pepper

Bread sauce (see p.218), to serve

Preheat the oven to 200°C (400°F/Gas 6).

Heat the oil in a flameproof and ovenproof casserole dish (Dutch oven) over a medium heat. When the oil is hot, add the lardons and fry for 4–5 minutes until golden. Move the lardons to one side of the dish.

Add the onions and shallots and fry for 5 minutes until lightly golden. Sprinkle over the sugar and cook until the onions and shallots are lightly caramelised. Add the prunes, chicken stock and wine. Bring to the boil and cook for 5 minutes.

Season the chicken with salt and pepper and sprinkle the bay leaves on top. Brush liberally with the melted butter. Place the chicken on top of the vegetables in the casserole dish (Dutch oven) and put in the preheated oven. Cook, uncovered, for 45 minutes, basting occasionally with the cooking juices.

Cover with a lid and cook for 20–25 minutes more until the chicken is cooked and tender.

Meanwhile, make the bread sauce (see p.218).

Cut the chicken into 4 portions and divide between the serving plates. Add some vegetables to each plate and serve the bread sauce separately.

OVEN-BAKING

I love oven-baking my birds. Not only because oven-baked poultry recipes embrace a few of my all-time favourite classic poultry dishes, but also because it gives me a chance to make some pies and other dishes involving pastry. In most of these recipes, you'll have to do some preparatory frying, but then you put the lot in the oven and wait for the magic to happen. Add this technique to your poultry-cooking repertoire. I guarantee you'll soon be hooked.

Chicken with 40 cloves of garlic

Roasted garlic has a lovely sweet, mellow taste. This recipe is best made the classic way, which involves hermetically sealing the casserole dish (Dutch oven) with a strip of paste made from flour and water. This locks in the flavour of the garlic and gives the dish its distinctive character. All you need as accompaniments are some baby roasted potatoes and buttered spinach.

SERVES 4

1 x 1.5kg (3lb 3oz) chicken

2 sprigs of rosemary, leaves only

2 sprigs of thyme, leaves only

40 plump garlic cloves, unpeeled

2 tbsp olive oil

600ml (1 pint/2½ cups) white chicken stock (see p.21)

300ml (10fl oz/1¼ cups) dry white wine

4 tbsp plain (all-purpose) flour

4 tbsp water, mixed with 1 tbsp sunflower oil

Sea salt and freshly ground black pepper

Preheat the oven to 180°C (350°F/Gas 4).

Season the chicken liberally with salt and pepper and place in a large lidded ovenproof casserole dish (Dutch oven). Sprinkle over the rosemary and thyme, then add the garlic around the bird. Pour over the olive oil, stock and wine.

Mix together the flour with the water and sunflower oil to form a paste and roll this into a long strip 5mm (¼in) thick. Press the paste strip around the edge of the casserole dish (Dutch oven), then cover with the lid to form a hermetic seal.

Place the dish in the preheated oven and bake for 1¼ hours, or until the chicken is tender and the juices run clear when the thigh is pierced with a skewer or small sharp knife.

To serve, carefully lift out the cooked chicken and remove the garlic. Strain the cooking juices through a fine sieve (strainer) into a small pan.

Cut the chicken into 8 pieces (see p.26) and arrange the garlic around the bird. Pour over the cooking juices and serve immediately.

Smoked chicken and madeira pies
with a jerusalem artichoke gratin

Here are some classic chicken pies, but with a twist. I've made them with smoked chicken together with pancetta, button onions and Madeira. The Jerusalem artichoke gratin makes a deliciously creamy accompaniment and is baked in the oven along with the pies. Some sautéed girolle mushrooms would add the finishing touch.

SERVES 8

1 cooked smoked chicken, approx 1.5kg (3lb 3oz)

2 tbsp olive oil

10g (¼oz/¾ tbsp) unsalted butter

1 onion, chopped

1 garlic clove, crushed

1 carrot, chopped

1 celery stick, chopped

1 tbsp plain (all-purpose) flour, plus extra for dusting

150ml (5fl oz/⅔ cup) Madeira

700ml (25fl oz/generous 3 cups) brown chicken stock (see p.21)

2 sprigs of thyme

100g (3½oz) pancetta, rind removed and chopped

250g (9oz) button onions, peeled

1kg (2¼lb) prepared puff pastry

1 egg, lightly beaten

Sea salt and freshly ground black pepper

FOR THE GRATIN

10g (¼oz/¾ tbsp) unsalted butter, softened

1kg (2¼lb) large Jerusalem artichokes

500ml (16fl oz/generous 2 cups) whipping cream

Cut the chicken into breast and leg portions (see p.26) and remove the skin. Cut the meat into 2cm (¾in) cubes and set aside. Chop the carcass into 2.5cm (1in) cubes.

Heat 1 tbsp oil in a pan over a medium heat. When the oil is hot, add the chopped carcass and fry for about 10 minutes until golden. Add the butter, onion, garlic, carrot and celery. Cook for 15 minutes until the vegetables are caramelised and golden. Add the flour and mix well, then cook over a low heat for 2 minutes more to cook the flour.

Add the Madeira and stock. Add the thyme and simmer for 25–30 minutes until the sauce has thickened and reduced by half. Strain through a fine sieve (strainer) into a clean pan. Set the Madeira sauce aside.

Meanwhile, heat the remaining olive oil in a large frying pan (skillet). When the oil is hot, add the pancetta and fry over a high heat until crisp and golden. Add the button onions and cook for 5 minutes more, still over a high heat.

Add half the Madeira sauce, reduce the heat and simmer for 10 minutes until the onions are cooked. Add the diced chicken and simmer for 2 minutes more, stirring until the chicken and vegetables are thickly bound in the sauce.

To make the pies, roll out the puff pastry on a lightly floured work surface and cut it into eight 7.5cm (3in) circles and eight 11cm (4in) circles.

Lay the 8 smaller circles on the work surface. Spoon a generous portion of chicken mixture into the centre of each circle. Lightly brush the edges of the circles with beaten egg. Cover the mixture with the larger pastry circles and press the edges together to seal. Using the edge of a knife, create a decorative swirl effect on top of the pastry. Press lightly on the bottom edge to give a decorative effect. Brush with more beaten egg, then place the pies on a baking sheet and set aside.

Preheat the oven to 180°C (350°F/Gas 4) and liberally grease an ovenproof gratin dish with butter.

Peel the Jerusalem artichokes and cut into slices about 5mm (¼in) thick. Put in the buttered dish and season with salt and pepper. Pour over the cream to just cover the Jerusalem artichokes, then place in the bottom of the preheated oven. Put the pies in the oven on the top shelf. Bake for 25–30 minutes until the pies and the artichoke gratin are golden.

A few minutes before you are ready to serve, reheat the remaining Madeira sauce over a gentle heat.

Serve the pies with a spoonful of the artichoke gratin and a drizzle of the reserved Madeira sauce.

Caribbean baked chicken paella

Sofritos form the basis of many Spanish Caribbean dishes. They are simply a combination of sautéed onion, garlic, red peppers (bell peppers) and garlic. There are many variations – for instance you could add some tomatoes and coriander (cilantro). When making this dish, it is important that, once you've added the stock, you do not disturb the paella by stirring it.

SERVES 6

6 tbsp olive oil

2 onions, chopped

4 garlic cloves, crushed

3 red peppers (bell peppers), grilled (broiled), skin discarded and flesh cut into strips

1 tsp red chilli powder

½ tsp dried oregano

1 x 200g (7oz) can chopped tomatoes in juice

1 tbsp tomato purée (paste)

1.2 litres (2 pints/5 cups) white chicken stock (see p.21)

200ml (7fl oz/scant 1 cup) coconut milk

2 good pinches of saffron strands

8 unboned chicken thighs, skin on

2 small bay leaves

100g (3½oz) cooking chorizo, skin removed and cut into 5mm (¼in) slices

1 tsp hot Spanish paprika (or to taste)

400g (14oz/generous 1¾ cups) Spanish paella rice, rinsed in cold water

100g (3½oz/generous ¾ cup) frozen peas

Sea salt and freshly ground black pepper

2 tbsp chopped coriander (cilantro), to serve

Preheat the oven to 170°C (325°F/Gas 3). To make the sofrito, heat 2 tbsp oil in a pan over a medium heat. When the oil is hot, add the onions, garlic, 1 red pepper (bell pepper), the chilli powder, oregano, tomatoes and the tomato purée (paste). Cook for about 5 minutes until the sofrito has softened and has a pulpy consistency. Set aside.

Put the chicken stock, coconut milk and saffron in a clean pan and bring to the boil. Reduce the heat and keep at a simmer.

Put 2 tbsp oil in a large heavy-based pan over a medium heat. When the oil is hot, add the chicken thighs and fry for 5 minutes on each side until golden and crispy. Remove with a slotted spoon to a plate.

Add the bay leaves and chorizo to the pan and cook the chorizo for 2 minutes on each side. Add to the chicken on the plate and set aside.

Heat the remaining 2 tbsp oil in an ovenproof pan. When the oil is hot, add the prepared sofrito and fry for 1 minute. Add the paprika, rice, peas and remaining red peppers (bell peppers). Stir to coat everything with the sofrito.

Add the chicken and chorizo, and their juices. Stir in the hot stock, add a little salt and pepper, and bring to the boil. Cover with foil and place in the preheated oven.

Cook for 15 minutes, or until the rice is tender and nearly all the cooking liquid has been absorbed.

Remove from the oven and adjust the seasoning. Sprinkle over the coriander (cilantro) and serve immediately.

Open chicken tortes *with mediterranean bagna cauda*

I first tasted a dish similar to this while in the South of France on a mystery stop eating tour. I loved the flavours: they were redolent of that entire part of France. Once I was home, I just had to recreate the experience. Here I make four individual tarts but if you prefer, you could make one large one in a big cake tin. I like to serve this with a fennel purée.

SERVES 4

6 tbsp olive oil

4 x 150g (5½oz) skinless, boneless chicken breasts

1 large aubergine (eggplant), halved lengthways and each half cut into 8 thick slices

2 courgettes (zucchini), thickly sliced

25g (scant 1oz/1¾ tbsp) unsalted butter, softened, for greasing

300g (11oz) prepared puff pastry

Plain (all-purpose) flour, for dusting

Sea salt and freshly ground black pepper

Small basil leaves, to serve

FOR THE BAGNA CAUDA

125ml (4½fl oz/½ cup) olive oil

2 large garlic cloves, crushed

1 small red chilli, deseeded and finely chopped

8 sunblush tomatoes, finely chopped

6 anchovy fillets in oil, rinsed, drained and chopped

1 tbsp pitted and chopped black olives

Squeeze of lemon juice

Heat 1 tbsp oil in a large frying pan (skillet) over a medium-high heat. When the oil is hot, add the chicken breasts. Cook for 1–2 minutes on each side until golden outside but still uncooked inside. Remove from the pan and allow to cool. Cut into 8 neat slices and set aside.

Add the remaining oil to the pan, then add the aubergine (eggplant). Cook for 5–6 minutes, or until the aubergine (eggplant) is soft. Remove with a slotted spoon and transfer to a plate covered with kitchen paper (paper towels) to drain.

Add the courgettes (zucchini) to the pan and cook for 5 minutes until soft.

Remove with a slotted spoon and transfer to a plate covered with kitchen paper (paper towels) to drain.

Preheat the oven to 200°C (400°F/Gas 6) and liberally grease the bottom and sides of 4 deep tart tins with the butter.

Arrange alternating slices of chicken breast, aubergine (eggplant) and courgettes (zucchini) in a neat overlapping pattern in the tins. Season liberally with salt and pepper.

Roll out the puff pastry on a lightly floured work surface and cut into 4 circles using a cutter slightly larger than the diameter of the tins.

Cover the chicken and vegetables with the pastry circles, tucking the edges of the pastry down the sides of the tins. Prick the pastry with a fork to allow steam to escape.

Place the tins on a baking sheet and bake in the preheated oven for 15–20 minutes, or until the pastry is crisp and golden.

Meanwhile, prepare the bagna cauda. Heat the oil in a small pan over a medium heat. When the oil is hot, add the garlic, chilli and tomatoes. Fry for 2–3 minutes, then stir in the anchovy fillets and olives. Add the lemon juice and season with salt and pepper.

Remove the tarts from the oven, and allow to cool slightly. Unmould onto 4 individual plates. To serve, drizzle over some bagna cauda and scatter with basil leaves.

Yogurt-baked chicken *with cumin, mint and green rice*

Cooking poultry and other meats in yogurt has been popular in areas like the Middle East and Asia for centuries. It helps to keep the meat moist and succulent. This impressive dish is great placed on the table straight from the oven for your guests to help themselves.

SERVES 4

2 tbsp olive oil

2 onions, thinly sliced

2 garlic cloves, crushed

1 tsp ground cumin

½ tsp ground cinnamon

4 chicken breasts on the bone

300ml (10fl oz/1¼ cups) Greek-style natural yogurt

2 eggs, lightly beaten

3 tbsp plain (all-purpose) flour

Good pinch of dried cloves

2 tsp dried mint

2 tbsp grated Parmesan cheese

150g (5½oz) cooked spinach, finely chopped

200g (7oz/1 cup) (raw weight) long-grain basmati rice, cooked

Sea salt and freshly ground black pepper

Lemon halves, to garnish (optional)

Preheat the oven to 180°C (350°F/Gas 4).

Heat the oil in a large shallow flameproof and ovenproof casserole dish (Dutch oven) over a medium heat.

When the oil is hot, add the onions, garlic, cumin and cinnamon. Reduce the heat and cook over a gentle heat for 10–15 minutes until golden. Remove with a slotted spoon to a plate.

Add the chicken breasts to the dish and cook for 3–4 minutes until golden on both sides. Return the onion mixture to the dish.

In a bowl, mix together the yogurt, eggs, flour, cloves and mint. Season with salt and pepper and combine well.

Pour the yogurt mixture over the chicken and onions, ensuring the chicken pieces are just covered.

Sprinkle over the Parmesan and place in the preheated oven. Bake for 30–35 minutes, or until the yogurt sauce has set and the chicken is tender.

Meanwhile, make the green rice. In a bowl, combine the cooked spinach with the cooked rice. Season with salt and pepper.

Serve the chicken in the cooking dish with the green rice alongside. Garnish with lemon halves, if using.

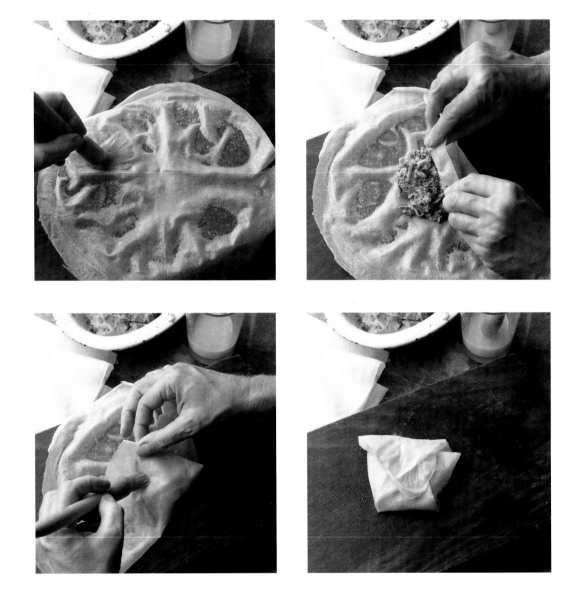

Guinea fowl pastilla

with ras el hanout roasted carrots and pomegranate yogurt

In this traditional Moroccan speciality, a whole pigeon is the preferred filling. In my recipe I use guinea fowl thighs, which produce game-like flavours that I think work rather well. Brik pastry, also known as warka pastry, is a thin, gossamer-like pastry made from flour and water. It can be sourced from Middle Eastern and French delis. You can replace it with filo pastry if you wish, but in that case, brush the pastry with melted butter instead of with beaten egg.

SERVES 6

6 guinea fowl thighs, skin on

1 onion, finely chopped

1 tbsp caster (superfine) sugar

2 tbsp orange flower water (optional)

2 small eggs, beaten, plus extra for brushing

50g (1¾oz/½ cup) ground almonds

6 sheets of brik pastry

Olive oil, for brushing

Sea salt and freshly ground black pepper

FOR THE MARINADE

1 tbsp chopped coriander (cilantro)

1 tbsp chopped flat-leaf parsley

1 small cinnamon stick

Good pinch of saffron strands

¼ tsp ground turmeric

FOR THE CARROTS

450g (1lb) baby carrots

1 tsp ras el hanout

2 tbsp olive oil

FOR THE POMEGRANATE YOGURT

1 pomegranate

100ml (3½fl oz/scant ½ cup) natural thick-set yogurt

TO SERVE

1 tsp icing (confectioners') sugar

1 tsp ground cinnamon

Micro coriander (cilantro) cress

The day before, place the guinea fowl thighs in a dish. Add the marinade – the coriander (cilantro), parsley, cinnamon stick, saffron, turmeric, and salt and pepper. Mix well, then cover with clingfilm (plastic wrap). Put in the fridge to marinate overnight.

The following day, heat a lidded heavy-based pan over a low-medium heat. When the pan is hot, add the marinated thighs and cook for 5–7 minutes until coloured.

Add the onion, sugar and orange flower water, if using. Add just enough water to cover the thighs. Cover with a lid, bring to the boil, then reduce the heat and simmer over a medium heat for 20–25 minutes, or until the meat is cooked and tender. Remove the thighs to a plate and leave to cool.

Return the liquid to the heat and cook until the sauce has reduced, and become thick and syrupy. Remove from the heat.

Quickly whisk the eggs into the sauce and cook them beyond the scrambled egg stage, until they become granular in texture. Remove from the heat and leave to cool.

Discard the skin and bones from the cooked thighs and shred the meat. Add the meat to the egg sauce and mix well. Stir in the ground almonds and season with salt and pepper.

Preheat the oven to 190°C (375°F/Gas 5).

To assemble the pastilla, liberally brush a sheet of brik pastry with beaten egg.

Divide the guinea fowl mixture into 6 equal portions. Lay one portion in the middle of a sheet of brik pastry, then fold the pastry over and over again to form a parcel (see p. 78). Brush with more egg to seal the edges.

Prepare all 6 pastillas the same way. Place on a baking sheet and brush with oil. Bake in the preheated oven for 20–25 minutes until golden and crispy.

Meanwhile, prepare the carrots. Toss the carrots and the ras el hanout in the oil in an ovenproof dish. Put in the oven with the pastillas and roast for 15–18 minutes until the carrots are tender.

Prepare the pomegranate yogurt. Cut the pomegranate in half and hold each half cut side down over a bowl of water. Tap the top of the pomegranate very hard with a rolling pin. The seeds will drop to the bottom of the water and the pith will float to the top.

Remove the pith and drain the pomegranate seeds well. Mix with the yogurt, season with salt and pepper and set aside.

Remove the carrots and pastillas from the oven. Dust the pastillas with icing (confectioners') sugar and ground cinnamon. Garnish with some micro coriander (cilantro) cress and serve with the carrots and a dollop of pomegranate yogurt.

Squab pigeon and rump steak pie

Pie-making is a truly great pastime. This pie combines the classic steak with young pigeon, cooked in red wine with girolle mushrooms. Try it – you won't be disappointed. Serve with hot buttery mash and you will have a really comforting, winter-warming dish.

SERVES 4–6

1.2kg (2¾lb) rump steak, cut into 2.5cm (1in) cubes

2 tbsp plain (all-purpose) flour, plus extra for dusting

3 tbsp sunflower oil

25g (scant 1oz/1¾ tbsp) unsalted butter

2 shallots, finely chopped

300g (11oz) girolle mushrooms or button (white) mushrooms, cleaned

1 tsp thyme leaves

2 tbsp Worcestershire sauce

150ml (5fl oz/⅔ cup) red wine

850ml (1½ pints/3¾ cups) veal stock or brown chicken stock (see p.21)

6 plump young squab pigeons, divided into leg and breast joints

400g (14oz) prepared puff pastry

Egg wash, made from 1 egg, beaten

Preheat the oven to 200°C (400°F/Gas 6).

Toss the cubed steak in the flour. Put 2 tbsp oil in a large, lidded flameproof and ovenproof casserole dish (Dutch oven) over a medium heat. When the oil is hot, add the steak and cook for 3–4 minutes until golden brown all over. Remove with a slotted spoon and set aside.

Add the butter to the dish and when it is hot, add the shallots, mushrooms and thyme. Fry for 2–3 minutes until the shallots and mushrooms are tender.

Return the steak to the dish and add the Worcestershire sauce and red wine. Increase the heat, bring to the boil and boil for 2 minutes.

Add the stock and bring back to the boil. Cover with the lid and place in the preheated oven for 1 hour.

Meanwhile, heat the remaining oil in a frying pan (skillet). When the oil is hot, add the pieces of squab pigeon and fry for 4–5 minutes until golden all over.

Remove with a slotted spoon and add to the steak in the casserole dish (Dutch oven). Return the dish to the oven for 30 minutes more, or until the meat is tender. Remove from the oven and leave to go cold. Leave the oven on as you prepare the pies.

Roll out the puff pastry on a lightly floured work surface to about 5mm (¼in) thick.

Divide the cooled squab pigeon and steak mixture between 4 individual pie dishes or use 1 large pie dish.

Carefully place the pastry over the meat, then trim away the excess pastry from the edges with a knife.

Decorate your pies as you prefer, then brush with the egg wash. Make a hole in the centre of each pie to allow the steam to escape.

Place on a baking tray (cookie sheet) and bake in the oven for 20–25 minutes until the pastry is golden and crusty. Allow to cool slightly before serving.

A simple duck and chicken cassoulet

Cassoulet gets its name from the earthenware pot that it is traditionally cooked in. It is thought to have been created in a small village near Toulouse in France. I'm sure there are as many recipes for cassoulet as there are cooks who make it. Here is mine. The classic version uses a mixture of preserved (confit) meats baked with white beans and various types of French sausage. Here I've used a mixture of chicken and duck confits. A crisp green salad and a good spoonful of French mustard are the best accompaniments. Sheer heaven!

SERVES 6

400g (14oz/2¼ cups) white haricot beans, soaked overnight then drained

2 litres (3½pints/8 cups) water

1 onion

4 cloves

6 black peppercorns

Bouquet garni (thyme, bay leaf and parsley tied together with kitchen string)

3 garlic cloves

200g (7oz) belly pork (sidepork), rindless

4 confit duck legs (homemade – see p.162 – or bought)

4 confit chicken legs (homemade – see p.162 – or bought)

6 Toulouse sausages

6 slices of Morteau sausage

2 tbsp tomato purée (paste)

4 tomatoes, deseeded and cut into 1cm (½in) cubes

120g (scant 4½oz/generous 2 cups) fresh white breadcrumbs

Place the soaked white beans in a large heavy-based flameproof pan or casserole dish (Dutch oven) with the water.

Cut the onion in half and stick 2 cloves in each half. Add to the pan with the peppercorns, bouquet garni, garlic and belly pork (sidepork). Bring to the boil.

Remove any scum that floats to the surface, then simmer for 1½–2 hours. The cooking time will vary according to the freshness of the beans. Do not overcook them; they should still be fairly firm in texture.

Meanwhile, heat a dry frying pan (skillet) over a medium heat. When the pan is hot, add the duck and chicken confits. Fry for 4–5 minutes to seal the confits and release their fat. Add the Toulouse and Morteau sausage and cook for 5 minutes on each side. Remove the confits and sausage from the pan with a slotted spoon and set aside.

Preheat the oven to 170°C (325°F/Gas 3).

When the beans are cooked, drain, reserving the belly pork (sidepork) and the cooking liquid. Discard the onion, peppercorns and bouquet garni. Slice the cooked belly pork (sidepork) and set aside.

In a bowl, mix the cooked beans with the tomato purée (paste) and diced tomato. Add the reserved cooking liquid.

Brush a little of the fat that was released by the confit meats over the base of an earthenware cassoulet pot or ovenproof casserole dish (Dutch oven). Add one-third of the cooked bean mixture.

Top with the confit meats and sliced belly pork (sidepork). Add another third of the bean mixture then tuck in the Toulouse and Morteau sausage. Top with the remaining bean mixture.

Lightly sprinkle with breadcrumbs, then transfer to the preheated oven and bake for 45–60 minutes until a crust has formed on top.

Remove from the oven, break the crust and stir the crust into the beans. Repeat this 3 or 4 times more until the cassoulet is cooked, about 1½–1¾ hours.

Increase the oven temperature to 180°C (350°F/Gas 4) and return the pot to the oven for 10–12 minutes until the top is golden and bubbling. Serve immediately.

SUMMER BARBECUE, GRIDDLING AND GRILLING

Nothing beats the flavour of succulent pieces of poultry cooked on a charcoal-laden barbecue, especially in the height of summer. Unfortunately, the weather isn't always on our side, but there's no need to despair. All the recipes that I give here can also be cooked on a ridged griddle pan. This cooks the poultry with bottom heat, like a barbecue, and the ridges in the pan give you the same charred grill lines that you get from the grill on the barbecue. And if you don't have either a barbecue or a ridged griddle pan, then have a go using overhead heat from a regular grill (broiler). All these methods are delicious.

Barbecue jerk chicken salad

The Anawak Indians were the first to marinate meats then slowly cook them over wood from the allspice tree to give them a spicy flavour. Jerk is a highly spiced marinade made from Scotch bonnet chilli peppers, which are tantalisingly hot and explode in your mouth. You could use a milder chilli if heat is not your thing. Here I combine the classic, hot-tasting jerk chicken with a lovely cooling summer salad.

SERVES 4

4 x 175g (6oz) boneless chicken breasts, skin on

½ Iceberg lettuce, chopped

1 small round lettuce, chopped

2 bunches of watercress, trimmed

2 firm ripe avocados, flesh cut into large dice

2 shallots, finely chopped

50g (1¾oz/¼ cup) drained sweetcorn (canned or frozen)

FOR THE MARINADE

4 tbsp sunflower oil

1 bunch of spring onions (scallions)

3 garlic cloves, crushed

2.5cm (1in) piece of root ginger, peeled and finely grated

2 tsp Scotch bonnet chilli pepper flakes

1 tsp ground allspice

½ tsp ground cinnamon

½ tsp dried thyme

2 tbsp **Worcestershire sauce**

½ tsp ground cloves

2 tbsp brown sugar

FOR THE DRESSING

1 tbsp white wine vinegar

3 tbsp olive oil

4 tbsp fresh orange juice

1 tsp grated orange zest

½ garlic clove, crushed

1 tbsp chopped coriander (cilantro)

The day before, make the marinade. Place the sunflower oil, spring onions (scallions), garlic, ginger, chilli pepper flakes, allspice, cinnamon, thyme, Worcestershire sauce, cloves and brown sugar in a blender. Blitz to a paste and transfer to a bowl.

Add the chicken breasts and rub all over with the marinade mixture. Cover with clingfilm (plastic wrap) and put in the fridge to marinate overnight.

The next day, light the barbecue or preheat a ridged griddle pan. When it is hot, remove the chicken breasts from their marinade, place on the grill (broiler) rack or griddle pan and cook for 8–10 minutes, turning them regularly until they are cooked through and charred on the surface. Remove from the heat and leave to cool slightly.

Meanwhile, make the dressing. In a bowl, whisk together the vinegar, olive oil, orange juice and zest, garlic and coriander (cilantro).

In another bowl, combine the lettuces, watercress, avocados, shallots and sweetcorn. Add a little of the dressing and lightly toss together.

Divide the salad between 4 individual serving bowls. Cut the cooked chicken breast into thick slices, place on top of the salad and serve immediately.

Korean skewered chicken with bibimbap

This Korean barbecued chicken dish features many of the key flavours of Korea's national cuisine – ginger, sesame oil, soy sauce and, one of my favourite discoveries of the year, gochujang, a spicy Korean sweet red chilli pepper paste. You can find it in Asian shops and markets. Typically these kebabs would be cooked over charcoal, but you can use a ridged griddle pan. Bimbimbap is a nutritious steamed rice dish with cooked and raw vegetables topped with egg, and drizzled with soy sauce and sesame oil.

SERVES 4

4 skinless chicken breasts, each cut into 8 large cubes

375g (13oz/1¾ cups) jasmine rice or basmati rice

600ml (1 pint/2½ cups) water

6 spring onions (scallions), cut into 2.5cm (1in) lengths

10g (¼oz/¾ tbsp) unsalted butter

300g (11oz) spinach leaves

100ml (3½fl oz/scant ½ cup) sunflower oil

4 free-range eggs

1 tbsp sesame oil, plus extra for drizzling

Sea salt and freshly ground black pepper

FOR THE MARINADE

2 tbsp gochujang paste, plus extra to serve

2.5cm (1in) piece of root ginger, peeled and grated

75ml (2½fl oz/5 tbsp) soy sauce

1 tbsp sesame oil

2 tbsp light brown sugar

TO SERVE

1 carrot, cut into fine strips

50g (1¾oz/½ cup) beansprouts

Micro cress

Soy sauce, for drizzling

For the marinade, in a bowl, mix together the gochujang paste, ginger, soy sauce, sesame oil and brown sugar. Add the cubed chicken and leave to marinate at room temperature for 2–3 hours.

Meanwhile, soak 8 bamboo skewers in cold water for 2 hours.

Light the barbecue or preheat a ridged griddle pan.

Make the rice for the bibimbap. Rinse the rice under cold running water until the water runs clear. Put the rice in a heavy-based pan with the 600ml (1 pint/2½ cups) water. The water should be the height of a finger joint above the rice. Stir well.

Bring to the boil and cover with a tight-fitting lid. Reduce the heat to medium and steam, undisturbed, for 15 minutes. Do not stir or uncover.

Turn off the heat and leave, undisturbed, for 10 minutes more.

Meanwhile, thread each skewer with alternating pieces of marinated chicken and spring onion (scallion). Cook for 3–4 minutes on each side until tender and charred.

Meanwhile, cook the spinach and fry the eggs. Put the butter in a pan over a medium heat. When the butter is hot, add the spinach and cook for 2–3 minutes. Remove from the heat and set aside.

Put the sunflower oil in a frying pan (skillet) over a medium heat. When the oil is hot, add the eggs, one at a time. Fry them sunny side up. Remove with a slotted spoon to a plate and cover with foil to keep warm.

Put the sesame oil in a pan over a medium heat. When the oil is hot, add the spinach and warm it through for a few minutes. Season with salt and pepper.

Fluff up the rice with a fork and divide it between the serving plates. Top each pile of rice with a fried egg. Place 2 kebabs on each plate and add some warmed spinach, and the carrot and beansprouts.

Garnish with micro cress. Drizzle over some sesame oil and soy sauce. Serve immediately with some more gochujang paste served separately.

Pollo fra diavolo

The devilled effect in this tasty Italian dish is achieved by adding lots of coarsely cracked black pepper and a good dousing of lemon juice. You'll get the best flavour by cooking the birds on a charcoal barbecue: it gives them a wonderful caramelised, smoky flavour. It was when I was in Italy a few years ago, that I first saw birds being barbecued under bricks. I was told it helped to cook them evenly. It's clever and it works, but if you haven't got any bricks or a barbecue, don't panic. The recipe is just as tasty if you use a ridged griddle pan. This dish lends itself to other types of poultry, too.

SERVES 4

4 double poussins, spatchcocked (see p.36), approx 500g (1lb 2oz) each

4 tbsp olive oil

Coarse sea salt

2 tbsp coarsely cracked black pepper

2 tbsp chopped oregano

1 tbsp chopped flat-leaf parsley

Juice of 2 lemons

2 lemons, halved, to garnish

300g (11oz/30 cups) rocket (arugula), to garnish

Put the poussins in a large shallow dish. Lightly coat both sides with oil and sprinkle with salt and black pepper. Sprinkle over the oregano, parsley and lemon juice. Leave to marinate at room temperature for 2 hours, covered with a clean tea towel (dishtowel).

Light a barbecue or preheat a ridged griddle pan. If using a barbecue, wrap 4 clean bricks in foil.

When the barbecue is hot, place the poussins on the grill (broiler) rack and top each with a foil-wrapped brick. Cook for 15 minutes until the poussins are cooked on the underside.

Remove the bricks, turn the poussins over and replace the bricks. Cook for 15 minutes more until the poussins are tender. Add the lemon halves, cut side down, and cook for a few minutes until a little charred.

If you are using a ridged griddle pan, cook the poussins for 15 minutes on each side.

Divide the poussins between the serving plates and pour over the cooking juices. Garnish with the lemon halves and rocket (arugula). Serve immediately.

Griddled duck confit
with potato and porcini galette, and sage jus

This impressive dish is not as hard to make as you might think. I use fresh porcini when they are in season in the autumn (fall), but dried, reconstituted porcini work well, too. You can also use a mixture of varieties of mushroom and if you are feeling extravagant, some sliced or chopped truffle added to the mushrooms will take this dish to new heights. Savoy cabbage cooked in a little duck fat would make a delicious accompaniment.

SERVES 4

4 tbsp duck fat

150g (5½oz) fresh porcini, cleaned and thickly sliced or 50g (1¾oz) dried porcini, reconstituted and thickly sliced

2 garlic cloves, crushed

2 shallots, finely chopped

2 tbsp chopped flat-leaf parsley

400g (14oz) starchy potatoes (such as Maris Piper or Desirée)

4 confit duck legs (homemade – see p.162 – or bought), removed from their fat

400ml (14fl oz/1¾ cups) brown chicken stock (see p.21)

25g (scant 1oz/1¾ tbsp) unsalted butter

8 small sage leaves

Sea salt and freshly ground black pepper

Heat 1 tbsp duck fat in a large frying pan (skillet) over a medium heat. When the fat is hot, add the porcini and fry for 4–5 minutes until cooked and golden, and the cooking liquid has evaporated.

Add the garlic, shallots and parsley and season with salt and pepper. Remove with a slotted spoon to a bowl and set aside.

Preheat the oven to 180°C (350°F/Gas 4).

Peel the potatoes and, using a mandolin slicer, slice them into a bowl in 3mm (⅛) slices.

Wipe the frying pan (skillet) with kitchen paper (paper towels), place it over a medium heat and add the remaining duck fat. When the fat is hot, add the potato slices and cook for 4–5 minutes until they soften slightly and become sticky and starchy. Season with salt and pepper.

Heat 4 individual 15cm (6in) tart tins one at a time over a medium heat.

When each tin is hot, arrange overlapping slices of potato to cover the base. Divide the porcini mixture between the tins, then cover with the remaining potato. Spoon over a little of the duck fat from the frying pan (skillet).

Press down on the potatoes with a spoon or fish slice to compress them, then place each tin over a medium heat for 7–8 minutes to brown the underside of the first layer of potato.

Transfer the tins to a baking sheet and place in the preheated oven. Cook for 15–20 minutes, pressing down on the top layer of potato from time to time with another pan.

Remove from the oven, unmould the galettes onto a plate, then slide them back into the tins the other way up. Return to the oven for 10 minutes more.

Meanwhile, preheat a ridged griddle pan.

When the pan is hot, add the duck leg confits and cook for 8–10 minutes, turning occasionally, until thoroughly heated through.

Meanwhile, make the sauce. Put the chicken stock in a small pan over a medium heat and bring to the boil. Boil rapidly until it has reduced in volume by half.

While the stock is boiling, put the butter in a small pan over a medium heat. When the butter is hot, add the sage and cook until the butter foams and becomes nutty in colour. Quickly whisk in the reduced stock and season with salt and pepper.

To serve, unmould the galettes onto the serving plates. Top each with a griddled duck leg confit and spoon over a little sage jus.

Dukkah chicken with lebanese bread salad

Dukkah is a Middle Eastern spice mix consisting of roasted hazelnuts and various seeds. It keeps for up to a month in an airtight container, so you could increase the quantities given here and use it for other purposes, too – sprinkled over chicken before roasting or over fish after grilling (broiling), for example. Sumac is a lemon-flavoured spice that is available from Middle Eastern stores.

SERVES 4

4 x 175g (6oz) skinless, boneless chicken breasts

2 tbsp olive oil, plus extra for drizzling

Sea salt and freshly ground black pepper

1 lemon, cut into 4 quarters, to garnish

FOR THE DUKKAH

75g (2½oz/½ cup) sesame seeds

3 tbsp cumin seeds

3 tbsp coriander seeds

50g (1¾oz/⅓ cup) hazelnuts, lightly roasted and skins removed

1 tsp sea salt

½ tsp cracked black peppercorns

FOR THE SALAD

4 Little Gem (Boston) lettuces, leaves separated

½ cucumber, cut into 1cm (½in) cubes

1 red pepper (bell pepper), halved, deseeded and cut into 1cm (½in) cubes

4 firm ripe salad tomatoes, cut into 1cm (½in) cubes

4 spring onions (scallions), chopped

4 radishes, thinly sliced

4 small pitta bread or Middle Eastern flatbreads

FOR THE DRESSING

Juice of 1 lemon

1 garlic clove, crushed

4 tbsp olive oil

Good pinch of sumac

2 tbsp chopped coriander (cilantro)

1 tbsp chopped mint

1 tbsp chopped flat-leaf parsley

Light the barbecue or preheat a ridged griddle pan, then prepare the dukkah. Place a dry frying pan (skillet) over a high heat and when it is hot, add the sesame, cumin and coriander seeds. Keeping the pan moving, toss the seeds until lightly toasted and fragrant.

Place the hazelnuts, toasted seed mix, sea salt and peppercorns in a small spice mill or coffee grinder. Blitz for 5–10 seconds to a coarse crumb texture. Pass the chicken breasts through the dukkah mix.

Brush the breasts with oil and cook for 4–5 minutes on each side until golden and cooked through.

Meanwhile, prepare the salad. Toss the lettuce, cucumber, pepper, tomatoes, spring onions (scallions) and radishes together in a bowl.

For the dressing, mix together the lemon juice, garlic, oil, sumac, coriander (cilantro), mint and parsley in another bowl. Season with salt and pepper. Toss with the salad. Toast the pitta bread.

Slice the chicken into 1cm (½in) slices and divide between the serving plates. Cut the pitta bread into fingers and add to the salad. Serve with the dukkah chicken drizzled with a little extra oil and garnished with lemon wedges.

Cambodian chicken drumsticks in banana leaves

Bananas are popular in Cambodian cooking and many dishes involve using their leaves to wrap meat or fish prior to griddling, barbecuing or roasting. The leaves help to keep the food moist as it cooks. The fun of giving your guests a banana-leaf parcel to unwrap on their plate is an added bonus.

SERVES 4

12 chicken drumsticks

Juice of 1 lime

12 x 15cm x 15cm (6in x 6in) banana leaves

12 Thai basil leaves

Sunflower oil, for brushing

Sea salt and freshly ground black pepper

Sweet chilli dipping sauce, to serve

Wedges of lime, to serve

FOR THE MARINADE

2 tbsp sunflower oil

2 tbsp caster (superfine) sugar

4 garlic cloves, crushed

2 onions, grated

4 tbsp ketchup manis (Indonesian sweet soy sauce) or light soy sauce

2 tbsp fish sauce (nam pla)

2 tbsp chopped coriander (cilantro)

½ tsp ground turmeric

The day before, make the marinade. In a shallow dish, mix together the oil, sugar, garlic, onions, ketchup manis, fish sauce, coriander (cilantro), and turmeric.

Score the flesh of each chicken drumstick with a sharp knife through to the bone so the marinade can penetrate the flesh. Add the drumsticks to the marinade, drizzle with lime juice and season with salt and pepper. Cover with clingfilm (plastic wrap) and put in the fridge to marinate overnight.

The next day, light the barbecue or preheat a ridged griddle pan.

Soften the banana leaves by blanching them quickly in a pan of boiling water for 5 seconds. Drain and wipe dry.

Place a drumstick in the centre of each softened banana leaf. Top with a leaf of Thai basil, then wrap the leaf around the drumstick. Secure the edges of the leaf with a cocktail stick (toothpick).

Brush the parcels with a little oil and cook for 25–30 minutes, turning frequently.

Divide the parcels between the serving plates so people can unwrap their own. Serve with sweet chilli dipping sauce and wedges of lime.

Miso griddled chicken
with aubergine, scented soy and green onions

Some of Japan's most inspired culinary products are made from soya beans, and miso is one of them. It is a rich savoury paste – white or dark – made by fermenting cooked soya beans with koji, a yeast-like mould. It is then left to mature from six months up to three years. In this tasty chicken dish, I use white miso paste as part of a simple marinade.

SERVES 4

4 large skinless, boneless chicken breasts, each cut into 6 large cubes

5 tbsp sunflower oil, plus 1 tbsp for greasing

2 large aubergines (eggplants)

1 cucumber, peeled and cut into 1cm (½in) slices

4 spring onions (scallions), cut into 5cm (2in) lengths

2cm (¾in) piece of root ginger, peeled and finely chopped

1 tbsp shoyu (Japanese soy sauce)

2 tbsp mirin (sweet rice wine)

1 garlic clove, crushed

2 tbsp coarsely chopped coriander (cilantro)

2 tsp sesame seeds, toasted, to serve

2 tsp walnut oil, for drizzling

FOR THE MARINADE

150ml (5fl oz/⅔ cup) light beer

50g (1¾oz) white miso paste

50g (1¾oz/¼ cup) caster (superfine) sugar

150ml (5fl oz/⅔ cup) shoyu (Japanese soy sauce)

1 tbsp sesame oil

4 tbsp sunflower oil

2 garlic cloves, crushed

Freshly ground black pepper

For the marinade, in a bowl, combine the beer, miso paste, sugar, shoyu, sesame oil, sunflower oil, garlic and pepper. Add the chicken cubes, cover with clingfilm (plastic wrap) and put in the fridge to marinate for 4 hours.

Soak 8 bamboo skewers in cold water.

Preheat a ridged griddle pan.

Remove the chicken from the marinade with a slotted spoon and thread on the skewers.

Brush the griddle pan with 1 tbsp sunflower oil and cook the skewers for 8–10 minutes, turning them regularly and basting with the marinade.

Meanwhile, cut the aubergines (eggplants) into thick slices or wedges.

Put the remaining 5 tbsp oil in a wok over a medium heat. When the oil is hot, add the aubergine (eggplant) and fry for 5–6 minutes until it begins to soften. Add the cucumber and spring onions (scallions) and cook for 2 minutes more.

Add the ginger, shoyu, mirin, garlic and coriander (cilantro). Toss together for 1 minute.

To serve, divide the aubergine (eggplant) mixture between the serving plates. Remove the chicken from the skewers and divide between the plates. Sprinkle over the toasted sesame seeds and drizzle with walnut oil. Serve immediately.

Chicken thighs with feta, lemon and oregano

I love the simplicity of this dish of great-tasting chicken marinated in a flavoursome mixture of olive oil, lemon and oregano. I like to serve the thighs on a bed of chargrilled young leeks, beetroot and courgettes (zucchini), then I drizzle the whole dish with a little sweet lemon dressing, which brings all the flavours beautifully together.

SERVES 4

1 quantity Olive Oil, Lemon, Mustard and Herb Marinade (see p.212)

8 large boneless chicken thighs

100g (3½oz) feta cheese

8 young leeks

4 small cooked beetroots, cut into large wedges

2 large courgettes (zucchini), thickly sliced

Sea salt and freshly ground black pepper

FOR THE DRESSING

Juice and grated zest of 2 lemons

75ml (2½fl oz/⅓ cup) water

2 tbsp caster (superfine) sugar

2 tbsp olive oil

Put the marinade in a large shallow dish and add the chicken thighs. Stir to coat the chicken in the marinade. Cover with clingfilm (plastic wrap) and leave to marinate at room temperature for a minimum of 4 hours.

Preheat 2 ridged griddle pans. When they are hot, add the marinated chicken thighs to one and cook for 6–8 minutes, turning them occasionally until the chicken is cooked through and the juices run clear. Two to three minutes before the end of cooking, crumble the feta cheese on top and return to the heat so the cheese melts.

While the chicken is cooking, add the leeks, beetroots and courgettes (zucchini) to the other griddle pan. Cook for 5–8 minutes, turning occasionally, until golden and lightly charred. Remove from the heat and season with salt and pepper.

Meanwhile, make the dressing. Put the lemon juice, zest, water and sugar in a pan over a medium heat. Bring to the boil. When the sugar has dissolved, remove from the heat and whisk in the oil.

Place a pile of griddled vegetables on each serving plate and top each with 2 chicken thighs. Drizzle with the dressing and serve immediately.

Two Japanese classics

If, like me, you are a lover of Japanese food, you will undoubtedly have enjoyed these two classics of the Japanese culinary repertoire. Both are cooked to melting tenderness. Yakitori is traditionally cooked on wooden skewers over charcoal, and basted in a sweet and savoury glaze. For the teriyaki marinade, the ingredients are simmered to reduce them before being used to marinate the poussins.

Japanese skewered chicken (yakitori)

SERVES 4

700g (1½lb) skinless, boneless chicken thighs

75ml (2½fl oz/⅓ cup) tamari (Japanese soy sauce)

3 tbsp sake (Japanese rice wine)

60ml (2fl oz/¼ cup) mirin (sweet rice wine)

1 tbsp caster (superfine) sugar

8 spring onions (scallions), cut into 2.5cm (1in) lengths

300g (11oz) shiitake mushrooms, halved

Sansho no kona (Japanese pepper flakes)

4 wedges of lime, to garnish

Soak 8 bamboo skewers in cold water for 2 hours.

Cut the chicken into bite-sized pieces and place in a bowl. Add the tamari, sake, mirin and sugar. Leave to marinate in this glaze at room temperature for 30 minutes.

Light the barbecue or preheat a ridged griddle pan.

Remove the chicken from the glaze with a slotted spoon and reserve the glaze. Thread the skewers with alternating pieces of marinated chicken, spring onion (scallion) and mushroom.

Cook for 8–10 minutes, brushing the skewers regularly with the reserved glaze until the chicken is cooked.

To serve, give the skewers a final brush with the glaze and sprinkle with the sansho no kona. Garnish with wedges of lime.

Teriyaki grilled poussins

SERVES 4

2 double poussins, approx 1kg (2¼lb) each, halved and boned

2 tbsp sunflower oil

4 wedges of lime, to garnish

FOR THE MARINADE

125ml (4½ fl oz/½ cup) shoyu (Japanese soy sauce)

2.5cm (1in) piece of root ginger, peeled and grated

2 garlic cloves, crushed

1 tbsp grated tangerine zest or orange zest

60ml (2fl oz/¼ cup) sake (Japanese rice wine)

Sea salt and freshly ground black pepper

To make the marinade, place the shoyu, ginger, garlic, tangerine zest, sake, and salt and pepper in a small pan over a low heat. Simmer for 5 minutes until the marinade has reduced and is sticky.

Place the poussin halves in a shallow dish and pour over the marinade. Leave to marinate at room temperature for 4 hours.

Preheat the grill (broiler). Remove the poussins from the marinade. Place on a rack set over the grill (broiler) pan; this will prevent the shoyu from caramelising too much.

Brush the poussins with oil. Grill (broil) for 12–15 minutes on each side, brushing occasionally with the marinade. To serve, spoon over the pan juices. Garnish with wedges of lime and serve immediately.

Griddled duck breasts
with green sauce and radicchio agrodolce

Serving cooked radicchio and other salad leaves rather than simply banishing them to the salad bowl is becoming more and more popular. The Italians have long appreciated cooked radicchio. The cooking removes some of the bitterness and adds a pleasant smoky flavour. Here I've made a radicchio *agrodolce* – sweet and sour radicchio.

SERVES 4
2 tbsp sunflower oil

1 onion, thinly sliced

2 tbsp balsamic vinegar

2 tbsp caster (superfine) sugar

100ml (3½fl oz/scant ½ cup) red wine

1 radicchio, shredded

4 x 180g (scant 6½oz) skinless, boneless duck breasts

Sea salt and freshly ground black pepper

FOR THE GREEN SAUCE
2 garlic cloves, crushed

25g (scant 1oz/1 cup) flat-leaf parsley

25g (scant 1oz/1 cup) basil leaves

2 anchovy fillets in oil

½ tsp Dijon mustard

50g (1¾oz) sweet dill pickled gherkins, finely diced

50g (1¾oz/6 tbsp) capers, rinsed and drained

2 tbsp white wine vinegar

6 tbsp virgin olive oil

FOR THE POTATO CAKES
450g (1lb) waxy potatoes (such as Charlotte)

25g (scant 1oz/1¾ tbsp) unsalted butter

2 tbsp olive oil

For the green sauce, place the garlic, parsley, basil and anchovy fillets in a mortar and crush to a pulp. Add the mustard, gherkins, capers, vinegar and olive oil, and season with salt and pepper. Set aside.

Next make the radicchio. Put 1 tbsp sunflower oil in a pan over a medium heat. When the oil is hot, add the onion, reduce the heat and cook over a low heat for 6–8 minutes until golden. Add the vinegar, sugar, wine and radicchio. Cook for about 15 minutes, still over a low heat, until the radicchio has caramelised. Set aside, covered with a lid, to keep warm.

Preheat a ridged griddle pan.

Meanwhile, make the potato cakes. Peel and grate the potatoes and squeeze dry in a clean tea towel (dishtowel). Season with salt and pepper.

Put the butter and olive oil in a small frying pan (skillet) over a medium heat. When they are hot, add ¼ tbsp grated potato and press down to flatten it. Fry for 6–8 minutes on each side until cooked through. Remove to a plate with a slotted spoon and cover with foil to keep warm. Repeat to make 4 more potato cakes.

Season the duck breasts with salt and pepper and brush with the remaining sunflower oil. Place the duck, skin side down, on the pan and cook for 4–5 minutes on each side if you like your meat rare, or 6 minutes if you prefer it well done. Remove from the heat and leave to rest for 5 minutes. Cut into thick slices.

Place a potato cake on each serving plate with a spoonful of radicchio. Top with the sliced duck breast, spoon over some green sauce and serve immediately.

Asian-style duck breasts *with cucumber and lychee salad*

In this dish I take the liberty of bringing together the cuisines of two countries – China and Japan. I use the breasts from a classic Peking barbecue duck in a salad that combines cucumber, lychees and coriander (cilantro). Then I dress the whole thing in a Japanese-inspired dressing.

SERVES 4

2 tbsp sticky rice

2 breasts taken from a Peking barbecue duck

FOR THE DRESSING

100ml (3½fl oz/scant ½ cup) rice wine vinegar

2 tbsp caster (superfine) sugar

4cm (1½in) piece of root ginger, peeled and thinly sliced

30g (1oz) pickled pink ginger

2 banana shallots, thinly sliced

2 red chillies, thinly sliced

2 tbsp mirin (sweet rice wine)

2 tbsp fish sauce (nam pla)

3 tbsp light soy sauce

1 tsp sesame oil

Juice of 4 limes

FOR THE SALAD

6 spring onions (scallions), cut into 1cm (½in) lengths

1 x 200g (7oz) can lychees, drained and halved

Handful of coriander (cilantro) leaves

½ cucumber, peeled and cut into thin strips

2.5cm (1in) piece of root ginger, peeled and thinly sliced

30g (1oz/1½ cups) mint leaves

1 red onion, thinly sliced

1 red chilli, thinly sliced

2 bunches of watercress

Preheat the oven to 180°C (350°F/Gas 4) and preheat a ridged griddle pan.

To make the dressing, put the rice wine vinegar and sugar in a small pan and bring to the boil. Transfer to a bowl and add the root ginger and pink ginger, the shallots, chillies, mirin, fish sauce, soy sauce, sesame oil and lime juice. Set aside.

Place the sticky rice on a baking tray (cookie sheet) and roast in the preheated oven for 20 minutes, turning occasionally, until lightly roasted.

When the griddle pan is hot, add the duck breasts and cook for 2 minutes on each side.

Meanwhile, prepare the salad. In a bowl, mix together the spring onions (scallions), lychees, coriander (cilantro), cucumber, ginger, mint, red onion, chilli and watercress.

Remove the duck from the pan and cut into thick slices. Add to the salad in the bowl.

Coarsely chop the roasted sticky rice.

To serve, drizzle over the dressing, divide between the serving plates and scatter over the roasted rice.

Griddled duck with tomato and olive antiboise dressing
and a silky goat's cheese mash

Named after Antibes in the South of France, antiboise dressing is very versatile. It is delicious with fish, shellfish and all types of poultry. I've included some coarsely cracked coriander seeds to add a pleasant crunch as well as delicious fragrance. This particular recipe is tasty served with a fresh green leaf and rocket (arugula) salad.

SERVES 4

4 x 175g (6oz) duck breasts, skin on

2 tbsp olive oil

Sea salt and freshly ground black pepper

FOR THE ANTIBOISE DRESSING

20 cherry plum tomatoes

12 small basil leaves

20 plump small black olives

1 small roasted red pepper (bell pepper), cut into 5mm (¼in) cubes

3 tbsp balsamic vinegar

6 tbsp olive oil

2 tsp coriander seeds, coarsely cracked

1 small red chilli, deseeded and finely chopped

2 garlic cloves, crushed

FOR THE MASH

600g (1lb 5oz) floury (mealy) potatoes (such as Desirée or Maris Piper)

100ml (3½ fl oz/scant ½ cup) double (heavy) cream

100g (3½oz/scant ½ cup) soft goat's cheese

150g (5½ oz/⅔ cup) unsalted butter

Preheat a ridged griddle pan.

Season the duck breasts with salt and pepper and brush them all over with oil.

Cook the duck breasts for 8–10 minutes on each side until golden and tender but still a little pink on the inside. You can cook them a little longer if you prefer them more well done.

Meanwhile, prepare the mash. Peel the potatoes, cut into chunks and put in a pan with salt and cold water to cover. Bring to the boil, then reduce the heat and simmer until tender. Drain and when cool enough to handle, peel and mash to a purée with a masher or pass through a potato ricer.

Put the cream in a pan over a medium heat and bring to the boil. Reduce the heat and stir in the hot potato purée.

Working as quickly as possible over a low heat, add the goat's cheese, then the butter. Beat until silky smooth. Season with salt and pepper. Set aside, covered with a lid, to keep warm.

When the duck is cooked, remove from the pan and leave to rest for 5 minutes.

Meanwhile make the antiboise dressing. Place the tomatoes, basil, olives, red pepper (bell pepper), vinegar, oil, coriander seeds, red chilli and garlic in a small pan over a low heat. Heat gently for 2–3 minutes.

Cut each duck breast into 6 cubes and divide between the serving plates. Add some mash to each plate, drizzle the duck with the dressing and serve immediately.

Quail burgers
with pancetta, chilli jam and herb mascarpone

I really love the contrast between the hot and spicy flavours of the chilli jam, and the coolness of the herb mascarpone in this recipe. Together with the burgers, they add up to a dish that is packed with flavour and intrigue. For maximum taste, cook the burgers on a charcoal barbecue. You can make the chilli jam in advance if you like and keep it in the fridge until needed. It makes a divine addition to any grilled (broiled), griddled or roasted poultry. Good, crispy chips will really complete your tasty burger.

SERVES 4

800g (1¾lb) skinless quail meat, coarsely minced (ground), then thoroughly chilled

1 large shallot, finely chopped

4 sage leaves, finely chopped

1 tbsp chopped flat-leaf parsley

1 egg yolk

2 tbsp olive oil

8 thin slices of pancetta

4 burger baps

50g (1¾oz) shredded Iceberg lettuce

2 tomatoes, peeled and thickly sliced

50g (1¾oz/5 cups) rocket (arugula) leaves

Sea salt and freshly ground black pepper

FOR THE CHILLI JAM

125g (4½oz/1⅔ cups) red chilli, roughly chopped

1 onion, roughly chopped

5cm (2in) piece root ginger, roughly chopped

125ml (4½fl oz/½ cup) rice wine or white wine vinegar

400g (14oz/2 cups) caster (superfine) sugar

100ml (3½fl oz/scant ½ cup) water

FOR THE HERB MASCARPONE

4 tbsp mascarpone

1 tbsp snipped chives

8 basil leaves, finely chopped

First make the chilli jam. Place the chilli, onion, ginger and rice wine or vinegar in a small blender and blitz to a coarse paste.

Place in a pan over a medium heat and add the sugar and water.

Bring to the boil, then reduce the heat and simmer for 10 minutes until the mixture becomes thick and jam-like in consistency. Remove from the heat and leave to go cold. Set aside.

To make the burger, in a bowl, mix together thoroughly the chilled quail meat, shallot, sage, parsley and egg yolk. Season with salt and pepper and return to the fridge.

Meanwhile, make the herb mascarpone. In a bowl, mix together thoroughly the mascarpone, chives and basil. Season with salt and pepper and set aside.

Light the barbecue or preheat a ridged griddle pan.

Divide the quail mixture into 4 evenly sized burgers. Brush liberally with oil and cook for 4–5 minutes, or according to taste.

While the burgers are cooking, add the pancetta and cook until crisp and golden.

Meanwhile, split the baps and toast the cut side.

Divide the lettuce and tomatoes between the bottom halves of the baps. Top with a quail burger and some rocket (arugula), then add a good spoonful of herb mascarpone, followed by a spoonful of chilli jam. Top each burger with 2 slices of griddled pancetta, cover with the top halves of the baps and serve immediately.

Barbecued squab pigeon
with gujarati spices and an everything green salad

Cooking squab pigeon over hot barbecue coals is the ideal way to prepare this dish, but a ridged griddle pan will do the job quite well. My accompanying salad is made with everything green, so 'everything green' seemed the natural name for it. Serve the spiced squab pigeon with some Indian-style flatbread, such as naan or paratha. This recipe makes a great starter or light snack.

SERVES 4

4 x 500g (1lb 2oz) squab pigeons, spatchcocked (see p.36)

Indian flatbread, such as naan or paratha

Sea salt and freshly ground black pepper

FOR THE MARINADE

3 tsp coriander seeds

2 tsp cumin seeds

½ tsp ground cinnamon

6 cardamom pods, split and seeds removed

½ tsp red chilli powder

2 garlic cloves, crushed

3 tbsp sunflower oil

1 small onion, finely grated

1 tsp tomato purée (paste)

Juice of ½ lemon

FOR THE DRESSING

Handful of coriander (cilantro) leaves

2 green chillies, deseeded and chopped

1 garlic clove, crushed

2cm (¾in) piece of root ginger, peeled and grated

1 tsp caster (superfine) sugar

Juice of ¼ lemon

1 tbsp Greek-style natural yogurt (optional)

FOR THE SALAD

Handful of baby spinach leaves

4 spring onions (scallions), finely chopped

50g (1¾oz)/1⅔ cups coriander (cilantro) leaves

20g (¾oz/1 cup) mint leaves

Handful of baby rocket/ arugula leaves

The day before, make the marinade. Heat a small dry frying pan (skillet) over a medium heat. When the pan is hot, add the coriander and cumin seeds and dry-fry for about 10 seconds until lightly toasted. Transfer to a small spice grinder or coffee grinder and grind to a powder.

Put in a blender with the cinnamon, cardamom seeds, chilli powder, garlic, oil, onion, tomato purée (paste), lemon juice and salt and pepper. Blitz to a paste.

Place the squab pigeons in a large shallow dish and rub all over with this paste. Cover with clingfilm (plastic wrap) and put in the fridge to marinate overnight.

The next day, light the barbecue or preheat a ridged griddle pan.

Remove the squab pigeons from the marinade with a slotted spoon and cook for 6–8 minutes on each side, until cooked through and charred on the surface.

Meanwhile, prepare the salad dressing and salad. Put the coriander (cilantro), chillies, garlic, ginger, sugar and lemon juice in the blender and blitz until smooth. Transfer to a bowl and stir in the yogurt.

For the salad, place the spinach, spring onions (scallions), coriander (cilantro), mint and rocket (arugula) in a large bowl. Add enough dressing to bind the leaves together.

Toast the flatbread and cut into quarters. Divide between the serving plates.

Top with the barbecued squab pigeons and a pile of salad. Add an extra spoonful of dressing alongside and serve immediately.

SAUTEING AND DEEP-FRYING

Sautéing is the starting point of many of the classic dishes in this book, but it's a cooking technique in its own right, too. You use a small amount of oil or fat in a shallow frying pan (skillet) over a relatively high heat. The poultry browns but keeps its texture, and all the moisture and flavour are locked in. In many of these recipes, you marinate the poultry before sautéing it, and sometimes you add other ingredients to the pan, to cook alongside the poultry. In deep-frying, you submerge the food completely in hot oil. It cooks quickly, so there's never any loss of flavour. Although deep-frying has had a bad press recently, there's no doubt that deep-fried food tastes good. Just don't eat it all the time.

Chicken sauté provençal

For me, this dish typifies the bright, fresh flavours of Southern France. Baby artichokes add a special flavour but you can use canned artichokes instead if you prefer. These don't need cooking though, so just make sure to add them near the end, giving them just a few minutes to heat through before serving.

SERVES 4

1.5–2kg (3lb 3oz–4½lb) chicken, cut into 8 joints (see p.26)

2 tbsp olive oil

2 garlic cloves, cut into thin slices

3 sprigs of thyme

2 small bay leaves

8 small artichokes (the smallest you can find)

8 spring onions (scallions), cut into 2.5cm (1in) lengths

75g (2½oz/scant ½ cup) Niçoise olives, pitted

2 anchovy fillets in oil, rinsed, drained and finely chopped

Juice of ¼ lemon

750ml (1¼ pints/3⅓ cups) brown chicken stock (see p.21) or veal stock

4 firm ripe tomatoes, skinned, seeds removed and cut into 5mm (¼in) dice

1 tbsp cornflour (cornstarch) (optional)

Sea salt and freshly ground black pepper

16 small basil leaves, to serve

Season the chicken pieces liberally with salt and pepper. Heat the oil in a lidded sauté pan or shallow flameproof casserole dish (Dutch oven) over a medium heat. When the oil is hot, add the chicken pieces and fry for 8–10 minutes, turning occasionally, until golden all over.

Add the garlic, thyme and bay leaves. Cook for 2–3 minutes more until the garlic has softened. Remove the chicken and herbs with a slotted spoon and set aside.

Return the pan to the heat. Cut the artichokes in half and add to the pan. Fry for 2–3 minutes, then add the spring onions (scallions), olives, anchovy fillets, lemon juice and stock. Bring to the boil.

Return the chicken and herbs to the pan and add the diced tomatoes. Reduce the heat and cover the pan. Simmer gently for 20 minutes, or until the chicken is tender and the sauce has reduced and thickened. If the sauce is a little thin, mix the cornflour (cornstarch) with a little water and whisk in just before serving.

Remove the thyme and bay leaves. Scatter with basil and serve immediately.

Chicken maryland revisited

During the 1970s, Chicken Maryland featured on every restaurant menu in London. Now, though, it's just a distant memory and hardly ever forms part of a chef's repertoire. I believe it's time for it to make a comeback, so here is my slightly updated version of the classic.

SERVES 4

4 x 175g (6oz) French-trim skinless chicken breasts (see p.16)

2 tbsp plain (all-purpose) flour

2 eggs, beaten with 1 tbsp water

75g (2½oz/1⅓ cups) fresh fine white breadcrumbs

100ml (3½fl oz/scant ½ cup) sunflower oil

75g (2½oz/5 tbsp) unsalted butter

4 small firm ripe bananas

Sea salt and freshly ground black pepper

Horseradish sauce (bought or homemade), to serve

FOR THE TOMATO JAM

4 firm ripe beefsteak tomatoes

25g (scant 1oz/1¾ tbsp) unsalted butter

1 sprig of thyme

1 tbsp clear honey

2 tbsp water

FOR THE CORN FRITTERS

100g (3½oz/scant ¾ cup) self-raising (self-rising) flour

1 egg

4 tbsp full-fat (whole) milk

150g (5½oz/ scant ¾ cup) sweetcorn kernels (canned or frozen)

First make the tomato jam. Blanch the tomatoes for 1 minute in boiling water, then drain and remove the skin. Cut in half horizontally and remove the seeds.

Put the butter and thyme in a lidded frying pan (skillet) over a medium heat. When the butter is hot, place the tomato halves, cut side down, in the pan. Add the honey and water, and cover with a lid. Cook for 10–12 minutes until the tomatoes are softened and lightly caramelised.

Remove with a slotted spoon to a chopping (cutting) board and chop finely. Return the tomatoes to the pan and set aside.

Season the chicken breasts with salt and pepper. Dip first in the flour, then in the beaten eggs, and finally in the breadcrumbs. Ensure the chicken is thoroughly coated in the breadcrumbs and brush off any excess.

Heat 75ml (2½fl oz/⅓ cup) oil and 25g (scant 1oz/ 1¾ tbsp) butter in a large frying pan (skillet) over a medium heat. When they are hot, add the chicken breasts and reduce the heat. Cook for 15 minutes over a low heat, turning occasionally, until golden and cooked through.

Meanwhile, make the fritters. In a bowl, mix together the flour, egg, milk and sweetcorn.

Heat the remaining oil in another frying pan (skillet) over a medium heat. When the oil is hot, drop spoonfuls of the sweetcorn batter into the oil. You may have to do this in batches.

Fry for 1–2 minutes on each side until golden, then remove and drain on kitchen paper (paper towels).

Wipe out the pan with some more kitchen paper (paper towels) and add the remaining butter. When it starts to foam, peel the bananas and cut in half lengthways. Add to the pan and fry until golden.

Quickly reheat the tomato jam.

Arrange 2 bananas halves on each serving plate and top with a chicken breast. Add 2–4 sweetcorn fritters, depending on size, and some tomato jam alongside. Serve immediately with the horseradish sauce separately.

Chicken sauté chasseur

This classic recipe is simple to prepare and tasty to eat. The sauce that the chicken is cooked in, with its scent of tarragon, is full of flavour. If you fancy a change, try substituting other types of poultry.

SERVES 4

1 x 1.5–2kg (3lb 3oz–4½lb) chicken, cut into 8 joints (see p.26)

2 tbsp plain (all-purpose) flour

2 tbsp olive oil

15g (½oz/1 tbsp) unsalted butter

2 shallots, finely chopped

300g (11oz/generous 3 cups) button (white) mushrooms or chestnut (crimini) mushrooms, thickly sliced

150ml (5fl oz/⅔ cup) dry white wine

100ml (3½fl oz/scant ½ cup) tomato juice

1 x 400g (14oz) can chopped tomatoes in juice

350ml (scant 12fl oz/1½ cups) brown chicken stock (see p.21)

2 tbsp chopped tarragon

Sea salt and freshly ground black pepper

Season the chicken joints with salt and pepper, then dip in the flour and shake off any excess.

Put the oil in a large lidded pan over a medium heat.

When the oil is hot, add the chicken joints and fry for 6–8 minutes, or until golden all over. Remove with a slotted spoon and set aside.

Add the butter to the pan and when the butter has melted, add the shallots and mushrooms. Cook for 5 minutes until the mushrooms have softened. Add the white wine, bring to the boil and boil for 2 minutes.

Add the tomato juice and bring back to the boil. Add the tomatoes and stock.

Return the chicken to the sauce and add the tarragon. Cover with a lid, reduce the heat and simmer gently for 25–30 minutes, or until the chicken is tender.

Serve immediately.

Chicken sauté marengo

Named by Napoleon's chef after the famous French victory at the battle of Marengo on 14 June 1800, this dish was the first I cooked as a young student chef at college some 40 years ago. It is a timeless classic and will always be a special memory for me on my personal culinary journey.

SERVES 4

1 x 1.5–2kg (3lb 3oz–4½lb) chicken, cut into 8 joints

2 tbsp plain (all-purpose) flour

4 tbsp olive oil

15g (½oz/1 tbsp) unsalted butter

200g (7oz/2 cups) button (white) mushrooms or chestnut (crimini) mushrooms, cleaned

1 tbsp cognac

150ml (5fl oz/⅔ cup) dry white wine

1 garlic clove, crushed

1 x 400g (14oz) can chopped tomatoes in juice

300ml (10fl oz/1¼ cups) brown chicken stock (see p.21)

100g (3½oz) cooked crayfish in brine, drained

Sunflower oil, for deep-frying

4 small free-range hen's eggs

8 x 1cm (½in) thick slices of baguette

Sea salt and freshly ground black pepper

1 tbsp chopped flat-leaf parsley, to serve

Season the chicken joints with salt and pepper, then dip in the flour and shake off any excess.

Put the olive oil in a large lidded frying pan (skillet) over a medium heat. When the oil is hot, add the chicken and fry for 8–10 minutes until golden all over. Reduce the heat, cover with a lid and cook for 18–20 minutes, or until the chicken is cooked.

Remove with a slotted spoon to a plate and set aside, covered with foil, to keep warm.

Pour off any excess fat from the pan and add the butter.

When the butter is hot, add the mushrooms. Cook for 5 minutes until golden. Remove from the pan with a slotted spoon and set aside with the chicken.

Add the cognac and white wine to the pan, bring to the boil and boil for 1 minute.

Add the garlic, chopped tomatoes and stock. Bring back to the boil and cook for 10 minutes until the sauce has reduced and thickened.

Return the chicken and mushrooms to the pan and add the crayfish. Stir well to combine. Remove from the heat and cover with a lid to keep warm.

Meanwhile, cook the deep-fried eggs. Heat the sunflower oil in a deep-fat fryer or deep pan to about 170°C (325°F). Carefully crack the eggs into the hot oil. (You may find it easier to cook 2 at a time and to crack them into a cup or glass before adding them to the oil.)

Fry for 2 minutes until set, golden and crispy, then remove with a slotted spoon to kitchen paper (paper towels) to drain.

Preheat the grill (broiler) and toast the slices of baguette on both sides.

Divide the chicken and crayfish between the serving plates. Top each with 2 slices of toasted baguette and a fried egg. Sprinkle with parsley and serve immediately.

Chicken liver and porcini risotto with marsala

This is the ultimate risotto and believe me, I've made a few over the years. In fact, a risotto topped with flash-fried chicken livers in marsala sauce was one of the first dishes I made when I was a young chef. It is important to clean the chicken livers thoroughly before cooking to remove any fatty or green traces, which can make them bitter. And it is also important to add the hot stock very gradually and keep an eye on the risotto the whole time you are cooking it.

SERVES 4

250ml (8fl oz/1 cup) Marsala wine

250ml (8fl oz/1 cup) brown chicken stock (see p.21)

1.75 litres (3 pints/scant 7½ cups) white chicken stock (see p.21)

4 tbsp olive oil

60g (2oz/4 tbsp) unsalted butter

120g (scant 4½oz) fresh porcini, cleaned and sliced or 50g (1¾oz) dried porcini, soaked for 1 hour in water, then drained and dried

1 shallot or 1 small onion, chopped

350g (12oz/1⅔ cups) carnaroli rice or other risotto rice

250g (9oz) chicken livers, trimmed

Sea salt and freshly ground black pepper

First make the marsala sauce. Put the Marsala and brown chicken stock in a pan over a medium heat. Bring to the boil, then reduce the heat and simmer for 15–20 minutes until the sauce has reduced by half and is thick and syrupy. Set aside.

While the sauce is cooking, place the white chicken stock in a pan over a low heat and bring to a simmer. Keep it simmering while you prepare the risotto.

Heat half the oil and 30g (1oz/2 tbsp) butter in a heavy-based pan over a medium heat. When they are hot, add the porcini and shallot and fry, stirring occasionally, for 4–5 minutes until lightly golden.

Add the rice and stir for 1 minute, until all the grains are coated in the fat.

Start adding the hot stock, a ladleful at a time. Wait until each ladleful has been absorbed before adding the next. Continue adding the stock in this way until the rice is just cooked al dente, then remove from the heat. Season with salt and pepper and stir in the remaining butter. Divide between the serving plates.

Quickly heat the remaining oil in a large frying pan (skillet). When the oil is hot, season the chicken livers with salt and pepper, and add to the pan.

Fry over a high heat for 1 minute, stirring occasionally, until golden.

Drain off the excess fat from the pan and add the marsala sauce. Mix together thoroughly.

Spoon some chicken livers and sauce onto each plate of risotto and serve immediately.

Pasta with chicken and spicy cacio e pepe sauce

This is my variation on the traditional Roman *cacio e pepe* (literally 'cheese and pepper') pasta dish. Here I've used fresh chicken but I often make it using leftover cooked chicken. I usually use a noodle-type pasta, like spaghetti or linguine, but you can use any pasta that you happen to have in your cupboard.

SERVES 4

400g (14oz) spaghetti or linguine (fresh or dried)

2 tbsp olive oil

2 garlic cloves, crushed

6 anchovy fillets in oil, rinsed, drained and finely chopped

¼ tsp dried red chilli (red pepper) flakes

1 small red pepper (bell pepper), halved, deseeded and cut into 5mm (¼in) cubes

120g (scant 4½oz) sunblush tomatoes in oil, drained and chopped

1 tsp finely crushed black peppercorns

1 tsp pink peppercorns in brine, drained

1 tbsp chopped oregano

4 x 150g (5½oz) skinless, boneless chicken breasts, cut into 2.5cm (1in) cubes

125g (4½oz/1 cup) Pecorino Romano, grated

Salt

Bring a large pan of boiling salted water to the boil over a medium heat. Add the pasta, bring the water back to the boil, then reduce the heat and cook, uncovered, until the pasta is al dente. This will take 6–9 minutes if you are using dried pasta; 3–5 minutes if using fresh. Drain in a colander.

Meanwhile, put the oil in a large lidded frying pan (skillet) over a medium heat. When the oil is hot, add the garlic, anchovy fillets, red chilli (red pepper) flakes, red pepper (bell pepper) and sunblush tomatoes.

Cook for 5 minutes, then add the black and pink peppercorns. Mix well then add the oregano followed by the cubed chicken. Cover with the lid and cook for 6–8 minutes until the chicken is cooked through.

Add the drained pasta and half the Pecorino Romano. Toss well until the pasta is well coated with the chicken and sauce. Divide the mixture between the serving plates and sprinkle with the remaining Pecorino Romano. Serve immediately.

Confit chicken
and griddled vegetable salad with anchovy and caper vinaigrette

The salad accompanying the confit chicken legs in this dish has all the hallmarks of summer. It is packed full of gutsy flavours and has interesting, slightly smoky overtones. I have used chicken legs, but you could use any other confit poultry.

SERVES 4

1 courgette (zucchini), sliced lengthways into 15mm (½in) slices

1 butternut squash, peeled and cut into 15mm (½in) wedges

1 small aubergine (eggplant), cut into 15mm (½in) slices

1 small red pepper (bell pepper), halved, deseeded and cut into 2.5cm (1in) cubes

6 tbsp olive oil

4 confit chicken legs (homemade – see p.162 – or bought)

50g (1¾oz) Parmesan cheese, thinly shaved

100g (3½oz) continental salad leaves

2 tbsp toasted pine nuts

Sea salt and freshly ground black pepper

FOR THE VINAIGRETTE

8 anchovy fillets in oil, rinsed, drained and coarsely chopped

Juice of ½ lemon

5 tbsp olive oil

2 tbsp superfine capers, rinsed

Preheat a large ridged griddle pan.

Place the courgette (zucchini), squash, aubergine (eggplant) and red pepper (bell pepper) in a large bowl. Add the oil and season with salt and pepper.

Cook the vegetables for 5–6 minutes on each side, or until cooked through and golden. Remove to a plate and cover with foil to keep warm.

Meanwhile, heat a large dry frying pan (skillet) over a medium heat. Remove the confit chicken legs from their fat and, when the pan is hot, add to the pan, skin side down. Fry for 5–8 minutes until the skin is crisp and golden and the chicken is heated through.

Meanwhile, make the vinaigrette. Place the anchovy fillets in a bowl with the lemon juice and oil. Whisk together until the vinaigrette has emulsified, then add the capers and season with salt and pepper.

Cut the vegetables into large pieces and place in a bowl. Add the vinaigrette and half the Parmesan, and toss together.

Scatter the salad leaves over the serving plates and spoon over the warm dressed vegetables. Top each plate with a confit chicken leg. Sprinkle over the pine nuts and scatter with the remaining Parmesan. Serve immediately.

Sautéed guinea fowl *with rosemary, anchovies, garlic and capers*

In this Italian-inspired dish, the guinea fowl has a piquant overtone that is the result of adding capers and anchovy fillets. It is quick to prepare, inexpensive, and always a winner whenever I make it at home. I recommend serving it with sauté potatoes and French (green) beans.

SERVES 4

8 guinea fowl thighs

8 guinea fowl drumsticks

3 tbsp olive oil

8 garlic cloves

1 tbsp coarsely chopped rosemary

150ml (5fl oz/⅔ cup) dry white wine

2 tbsp balsamic vinegar

400ml (14fl oz/1¾ cups) brown chicken stock (see p.21)

4 anchovy fillets in oil, rinsed, drained and chopped

2 tbsp capers, rinsed and drained

Sea salt and freshly ground black pepper

Make 3 incisions in each of the guinea fowl pieces with a sharp knife. Season with salt and pepper.

Heat the oil in a large frying pan (skillet) over a medium heat. When the oil is hot, add the pieces of guinea fowl. Reduce the heat and cook over a low heat, turning occasionally, for 15–20 minutes until golden brown.

Add the garlic and rosemary and cook for 5 minutes more until the garlic is lightly caramelised.

Add the wine and vinegar, increase the heat and bring to the boil.

Add the stock, anchoy fillets and capers. Reduce the heat and simmer gently for 10 minutes until the guinea fowl is cooked and tender. Serve immediately.

Chicken escalope *with apple, black pudding, girolles and mustard*

This dish is not only delicious and simple to cook, but once you have prepared your chicken escalope (scallop), it cooks very quickly. The Pedro Ximénez sherry that features here is a delight and I use it a lot in my cooking. I love its nice syrupy consistency and its sweet flavour. If you can't get hold of it it, you can substitute any sweet sherry.

SERVES 4

4 x 175g (6oz) skinless, boneless chicken breasts

75g (2½oz/5 tbsp) unsalted butter

175g (6oz) girolle mushrooms, wiped and trimmed

1 shallot, finely chopped

2 sprigs of thyme

100ml (3½fl oz/scant ½ cup) Pedro Ximénez sherry or other sweet sherry

150ml (5fl oz/⅔ cup) brown chicken stock (see p.21)

1 tsp Dijon mustard

1 tbsp crème fraîche

8 x 1cm (½in) thick slices of black pudding (blood sausage), skin removed

2 Granny Smith apples

Sea salt and freshly ground black pepper

Flatten the chicken breasts to a thickness of about 5mm (¼in) (see below).

Put half the butter in a large frying pan (skillet) over a medium heat. When the butter is hot, season the escalopes (scallops) with salt and pepper and add to the pan. Cook for 3–4 minutes on each side. You may need to do this in 2 batches. Remove to a plate with a slotted spoon and cover with foil to keep warm.

Increase the heat under the pan, then add the mushrooms. Fry for 5 minutes until golden, then add the shallot and thyme. Cook for 2 minutes.

Add the sherry and stock, and bring to the boil. Boil for 2–3 minutes, or until the liquid has reduced by half. Add the mustard and crème fraîche. Season the sauce with salt and pepper and set aside.

Meanwhile, heat the remaining butter in a clean frying pan (skillet) over a medium heat. When the butter is hot, add the black pudding (blood sausage) and fry for 2 minutes on each side. Remove with a palette knife to a plate and cover with foil to keep warm.

Peel and core the apples and cut them horizontally into thin slices. Add to the pan and fry for a couple of minutes, turning occasionally, until golden.

Return the chicken escalopes (scallops) and mushrooms to the sauce and heat through gently for a few minutes.

Divide between the serving plates and arrange the black pudding (blood sausage) and apple slices alongside. Serve immediately.

Preparing a poultry escalope (scallop)

Remove the bone from the poultry breast. Place the breast on a sheet of clingfilm (plastic wrap), then top with another sheet. Use a cutlet bat (shown here), meat tenderiser or rolling pin, hit the breast all over to flatten it to an even thickness of about 5mm (¼in).

Sauté chicken *with smoked paprika, chorizo and smoked almonds*

The dish is redolent with flavours from Spain. I adore the smoky notes of the sauce that come from including *pimentón* – Spanish smoked paprika. Serve this chicken with saffron rice; it makes the ideal accompaniment.

SERVES 4

8 chicken leg portions, cut into thighs and drumsticks

2 tsp smoked paprika (pimentón)

2 tbsp olive oil

150g (5½oz) cooking chorizo, skin removed and cut into 2cm (¾in) slices

2 red peppers (bell peppers), halved, deseeded and cut into strips

1 green pepper (bell pepper), halved, deseeded and cut into strips

2 garlic cloves, crushed

100ml (3½fl oz/scant ½ cup) dry white wine

1 tbsp tomato purée (paste)

⅓ tsp dried red chilli (red pepper) flakes

200ml (7fl oz/scant 1 cup) tomato juice or passata

150ml (5fl oz/⅔ cup) brown chicken stock (see p.21)

Sea salt and freshly ground black pepper

50g (1¾oz/⅓ cup) smoked almonds, to serve

1 tbsp chopped flat-leaf parsley, to serve

Season the chicken pieces with salt and pepper and with half the paprika.

Put the oil in a large lidded frying pan (skillet) over a medium heat. When the oil is hot, add the chicken pieces and chorizo. Fry for about 5 minutes on each side until both are golden brown.

Add the red and green peppers (bell peppers), the remaining paprika and the garlic. Reduce the heat, cover with a lid and cook for 10 minutes until the peppers are softened. Add the wine and bring to the boil. Boil for 2 minutes, uncovered.

Add the tomato purée (paste), chilli (red pepper) flakes, tomato juice and stock. Bring back to the boil, then reduce the heat.

Simmer, uncovered, for 20–25 minutes, occasionally turning the chicken in the sauce.

Scatter with smoked almonds and parsley and serve immediately.

Kung pao chicken

Kung Pao chicken – sometimes also referred to as Gong Bao chicken – is a legendary Sichuanese dish consisting of tender, marinated chicken pieces, lip-tingling spices and crisp roasted peanuts, all in a wonderful fragrant sauce. Serve it with simple steamed rice and stir-fried greens, such as bok choy or Chinese broccoli.

SERVES 4

4 x 175g (6oz) skinless, boneless chicken breasts

2 tbsp sunflower oil

75g (2½oz/½ cup) peanuts

1 tsp sesame oil

FOR THE MARINADE

1 tsp sea salt

2 tbsp light soy sauce

2 tbsp dry sherry or rice wine

2 tsp arrowroot or cornflour (cornstarch)

100ml (3½fl oz/scant ½ cup) white chicken stock (see p.21)

1 tsp caster (superfine) sugar

2 garlic cloves, thinly sliced

4cm (1½in) piece of root ginger, peeled and thinly sliced

4 spring onions (scallions), sliced

2 small red chillies, finely chopped

2 tsp chinkiang vinegar (Chinese black rice vinegar)

Cut the chicken into 1cm (½in) strips, then into small cubes. Set aside.

To make the marinade, mix together in a bowl the sea salt, soy sauce, sherry, arrowroot, stock, sugar, garlic, ginger, spring onions (scallions), chillies and vinegar.

Add the chicken cubes and leave to marinate at room temperature for 20 minutes.

Heat the sunflower oil in a wok or large frying pan (skillet) over a high heat. When the oil is hot, remove the chicken from the marinade with a slotted spoon, reserving the marinade. Add the chicken to the wok with the peanuts and stir-fry for 2 minutes. Remove with a slotted spoon to a dish. Set aside.

Add the reserved marinade to the wok and bring to the boil. Reduce the heat to a simmer.

Return the chicken and peanuts to the wok and cook for 2–3 minutes more.

Add the sesame oil and serve immediately.

Chicken with olives, preserved lemons and dates

I suggest using medjool dates for this dish. They are sticky and sweet, and just perfect for this Moroccan-inspired chicken dish. Some fluffy couscous makes a wonderful accompaniment.

SERVES 4

1 x 1.5kg (3lb 3oz) chicken, cut into 8 joints (see p.26)

2 tbsp plain (all-purpose) flour

3 tbsp olive oil

8 shallots, finely chopped

2.5cm (1in) piece of root ginger, peeled and finely chopped

½ tsp ground cumin

¼ tsp paprika

¼ tsp ground turmeric

2 tsp harissa paste

2 cinnamon sticks

3 preserved lemons, cut into wedges

750ml (1¼ pints/3⅓ cups) white chicken stock (see p.21)

Good pinch of saffron strands

12 small green olives, pitted

12 medjool dates, pitted and halved

2 tbsp chopped coriander (cilantro)

Sea salt and freshly ground black pepper

FOR THE COUSCOUS

600ml (1 pint/2½ cups) water

300g (11oz/1½ cups) couscous

25g (scant 1oz/1¾ tbsp) unsalted butter

Good pinch of ground cumin

Season the chicken joints liberally with salt and pepper, then dust generously with flour.

Put 2 tbsp oil in a large shallow sauté pan over a medium heat. When the oil is hot, add the chicken and fry for 5–6 minutes, turning occasionally, until golden all over. Remove with a slotted spoon and set aside.

Add the remaining oil to the pan, then add the shallots. Reduce the heat and cook, stirring, for 3–4 minutes until golden. Add the ginger, cumin, paprika, turmeric and harissa paste. Stir well.

Tuck in the cinnamon sticks and add the preserved lemons, stock and saffron. Bring to the boil, then reduce the heat.

Return the chicken joints to the pan and simmer for 15 minutes. Add the olives and cook for about 10 minutes more until the chicken is cooked and the juices run clear when the thickest part of a drumstick is pierced with a skewer or small sharp knife.

Meanwhile, prepare the couscous. Place the water in a small pan and bring to the boil.

Put the couscous, butter, cumin and salt and pepper to taste in a heatproof bowl. Add the boiling water and mix well with a fork.

Cover the bowl tightly with clingfilm (plastic wrap) and leave to steam for 5 minutes.

Remove the chicken from the pan and divide between the serving plates.

Return the sauce to the heat. Remove the cinnamon stick and add the dates. Heat through for 1 minute, then add the coriander (cilantro).

Remove the clingfilm (plastic wrap) from the couscous and fluff up with a fork.

Pour the sauce over the chicken and serve immediately with the couscous alongside.

Turkey piadini

Piadini are Italian-style flatbreads, similar to tortillas in thickness and size. This piadini recipe is my Italian take on Mexican fajitas. It is full of flavour and served with a crisp green salad, makes a great meal.

SERVES 4

600g (1lb 5oz) skinless, boneless turkey breasts, cut into 2.5cm (1in) cubes

3 tbsp olive oil

Juice of ¼ lemon

1 tbsp balsamic vinegar

Pinch of caster (superfine) sugar

Sea salt and freshly ground black pepper

FOR THE SALSA

2 ripe avocados

4 tomatoes, deseeded and cut into small cubes

1 green chilli, finely chopped

1 red onion, finely chopped

3 tbsp prepared salsa verde (see p.146)

TO SERVE

4 piadini (Italian flatbreads)

100g (3½oz) rocket (arugula)

100ml (3½fl oz/scant ½ cup) sour cream

Put the cubed turkey breast in a bowl and add 1 tbsp oil, the lemon juice, vinegar, sugar, and salt and pepper. Cover with clingfilm (plastic wrap) and leave to marinate at room temperature for 30 minutes.

Meanwhile, make the salsa. Peel the avocados and dice the flesh. In a bowl, mix together the tomatoes, chilli, red onion, avocado and salsa verde. Season with salt and pepper and set aside.

Put the remaining oil in a large frying pan (skillet) over a medium heat. When the oil is hot, remove the turkey from the marinade with a slotted spoon and add to the pan. Cook for 6–8 minutes until cooked through.

Meanwhile, lay the piadini on the work surface and scatter with some rocket (arugula).

Divide the turkey mixture between the piadini and top with some salsa.

Roll up the piadini and serve immediately with a generous spoonful of sour cream.

Balsamic mint duck breast
with honey-roasted squash and cavolo nero

Marinating duck breasts in a balsamic vinegar and mint sauce helps cut through the richness of the duck, as well as adding a lovely flavour and tenderising the meat. Cavolo nero (Tuscan kale), or black cabbage, is an Italian vegetable that is readily available but Savoy cabbage is just as good if you prefer. A celeriac or parsnip purée would be wonderful to accompany this dish.

SERVES 4

4 boneless duck breasts, approx 180g (scant 6½oz) each

75g (2½oz/5 tbsp) unsalted butter

1 butternut squash, peeled and cut into large cubes

2 tbsp clear honey

200ml (7fl oz/scant 1 cup) brown chicken stock (see p.21)

500g (1lb 2oz/3¼ cups) cavolo nero (Tuscan kale), cut into small pieces

Sea salt and freshly ground black pepper

FOR THE MARINADE

4 tbsp good-quality aged balsamic vinegar

1 tbsp clear honey

2 tbsp prepared mint sauce

1 tbsp prepared English mustard

Good pinch of ground cinnamon

The day before, make the marinade. In a bowl, mix together the vinegar, honey, mint sauce, mustard, cinnamon, and salt and pepper to taste.

Cut several slashes in each duck breast using a small sharp knife. Place the breasts in a large shallow dish. Add the marinade and stir to coat. Cover with clingfilm (plastic wrap) and put in the fridge to marinate overnight.

The next day, preheat the oven to 200°C (400°F/ Gas 6).

Place 20g (¾oz/1½ tbsp) butter in a small ovenproof frying pan (skillet) over a medium heat. When the butter is hot, add the butternut squash and brown it lightly.

Add the honey, then place the pan in the preheated oven. Roast for 6–8 minutes until the squash is cooked and lightly caramelised. Remove from the oven and cover with foil to keep warm.

Meanwhile, remove the duck from the marinade with a slotted spoon, reserving the marinade. Put a large dry frying pan (skillet) over a medium heat. When the pan is hot, add the duck and cook for 5–6 minutes on each side until caramelised. Remove from the pan, wrap each piece in foil and leave to rest for 5 minutes.

While the duck is cooking and resting, make the sauce and prepare the cavolo nero (Tuscan kale). For the sauce, add the stock to the pan together with 2 tbsp reserved marinade. Bring to the boil, reduce the heat and simmer for 5 minutes until thickened. Strain the sauce through a fine sieve (strainer) into a jug (pitcher). Cover with foil to keep warm.

Bring a pan of water to the boil then add the cavolo nero (Tuscan kale). Cook for 2–3 minutes, then drain and toss in the remaining butter. Season with salt and pepper.

Divide the cavolo nero (Tuscan kale) between the serving plates and place the honey-roasted squash alongside. Cut the duck into thin slices and arrange on the cavolo nero (Tuscan kale). Pour the sauce over the duck and serve immediately.

Devilled guinea fowl legs
with castelluccio lentils and watercress salsa verde

In this dish I 'devil' the guinea fowl leg confits, seasoning them with a spicy mix of mustard and paprika. Devilling meat has been a popular cooking technique for many years. The devilled meat is usually coated in breadcrumbs, too. You can prepare any type of poultry legs this way. The braised chicory and watercress salsa verde make great accompaniments.

SERVES 4

1 tbsp **D**ijon mustard

2 tbsp clear honey

½ tsp sweet paprika

4 confit guinea fowl legs, (homemade – see p.162 – or bought), removed from their fat

2 eggs, beaten

100g (3½oz/generous 1¾ cups) fresh white breadcrumbs

2 tbsp olive oil

20g (¾oz/1½ tbsp) unsalted butter

Sea salt and freshly ground black pepper

FOR THE SALSA VERDE

Small handful of watercress leaves

Small handful of flat-leaf parsley leaves

1 garlic clove, crushed

1 tsp capers, rinsed and drained

2 anchovy fillets in oil, rinsed and drained

2 tbsp red wine vinegar

6 tbsp olive oil

1 tsp Dijon mustard

FOR THE CHICORY

40g (scant 1½oz/3 tbsp) unsalted butter

8 small heads of chicory

2 tbsp caster (superfine) sugar

Juice of ½ lemon

150ml (5fl oz/⅔ cup) water

FOR THE LENTILS

50g (1¾oz/3½ tbsp) unsalted butter

1 carrot, finely diced

1 shallot, finely diced

1 celery stick, finely diced

300g (11oz/1½ cups) Castelluccio lentils or Puy lentils

600ml (1 pint/2½ cups) brown chicken stock (see p.21)

First make the salsa verde. Place the watercress, parsley, garlic, capers, anchovy fillets, vinegar, oil and mustard in a small blender and blitz to a coarse purée. (You can also make the salsa 2–3 days in advance and refrigerate in a sealed container.)

Preheat the oven to 180°C (350°F/Gas 4).

For the chicory, melt 10g (¼oz/¾ tbsp) butter in a small, lidded flameproof and ovenproof casserole dish (Dutch oven) over a medium heat. When the butter has melted, add the chicory and sweat for 1 minute. Add half the sugar, the lemon juice and the water. Cover with a tight-fitting lid and place in the preheated oven. Cook for 30–40 minutes, or until tender. Remove from the oven and leave to cool.

Meanwhile, prepare the lentils. Put 10g (¼oz/ ¾ tbsp) butter in a large lidded pan over a medium heat. When the butter has melted, add the carrot, shallot and celery and sweat for 5 minutes. Add the lentils and stock. Bring to the boil, then reduce the heat and simmer for 30 minutes, or until the lentils are just tender. Add the remaining butter and

season with salt and pepper. Remove from the heat and cover with a lid to keep warm.

In a bowl, mx together the mustard, honey and paprika. Brush the mixture liberally over the guinea fowl legs. Dip each leg into the beaten eggs, then into the breadcrumbs.

Put the oil and butter in a frying pan (skillet) over a medium heat. When they are hot, add the guinea fowl legs. Fry gently for 4–5 minutes on each side until golden all over.

Meanwhile, put the remaining butter for the chicory in a small frying pan (skillet) over a medium heat. When the butter has melted, add the remaining sugar and the chicory. Cook for 2–3 minutes until the chicory is heated through and lightly caramelised. Season with salt and pepper.

Divide the lentils between the serving plates and top with 2 braised heads of chicory and a guinea fowl leg. Serve immediately with the watercress salsa verde alongside.

Turkey escalopine
with asparagus, wild mushroom and hazelnut vinaigrette, and potato and reblochon mash

This is one of my favourite ways to use turkey breasts. Instead of being cooked whole in the usual manner, they are cut into thin escalopes (scallops). They take minutes to cook.

SERVES 4

4 x 160g (5½oz) turkey breast escalopes (scallops), approx 5mm (¼in) thick (see p.135)

1 egg, beaten with 2 tbsp water

50g (1¾oz/scant 1 cup) fresh white breadcrumbs

1 tbsp sunflower oil

12 tips of green asparagus

8 tips of white asparagus

15g (½oz/1 tbsp) unsalted butter

Sea salt and freshly ground black pepper

FOR THE VINAIGRETTE

1 tbsp olive oil

250g (9oz) wild mushrooms, cleaned

1 shallot, finely chopped

1 tbsp sherry vinegar

2 tbsp hazelnut oil

25g (scant 1oz/¼ cup) chopped roasted hazelnuts

2 tbsp snipped chives

FOR THE MASH

650g (1lb 7oz) floury (mealy) potatoes (such as Desirée or Maris Piper), unpeeled

60ml (2fl oz/¼ cup) full-fat (whole) milk

3 tbsp double (heavy) cream

150g (5½oz/⅔ cup) unsalted butter, chilled and cut into small dice

75g (2½oz/⅔ cup) Reblochon cheese, rind removed and grated

First make the mash. Bring a pan of water to the boil and add the unpeeled potatoes. Reduce the heat and cook for 25–30 minutes, or until tender. Drain the potatoes, leave to cool slightly, then peel. Pass through a potato ricer or fine sieve (strainer).

Put the milk and cream in a small pan over a low heat. When they are warm, add the potatoes. Mix together thoroughly, then beat in the butter. Add the cheese and beat until smooth and creamy. Season with salt and pepper and set aside.

Dip the turkey escalopes (scallops) in the beaten egg, then in the breadcrumbs. Make sure they are well coated in breadcrumbs and brush off any excess. Heat the sunflower oil in a non-stick frying pan (skillet) over a medium heat. When the oil is hot, add the escalopes (scallops) and cook for 4–5 minutes on each side until golden.

Meanwhile, prepare the asparagus tips and the vinaigrette. Blanch the asparagus tips in boiling water for 4–5 minutes, then drain thoroughly. Return to the pan and add the butter. Season with salt and pepper.

For the vinaigrette, put half the olive oil in a clean frying pan (skillet) over a medium heat. When the oil is hot, add the mushrooms and shallot. Cook, stirring occasionally, for 2–3 minutes until golden.

Add the vinegar and increase the heat. Add the remaining olive oil, the hazelnut oil, and the hazelnuts and chives. Season with salt and pepper. Cook for 2 minutes.

Meanwhile, reheat the mash over a low heat, stirring frequently.

Divide the escalopes (scallops) between the serving plates and drizzle with a spoonful or two of warm vinaigrette. Top with buttered asparagus and serve immediately with the cheesy mash.

Southern-fried chicken *with spicy fries and ranch mayo*

Purists may be surprised that I don't use chicken joints on the bone for this American stalwart, but instead prefer smaller pieces of chicken breast. If you make this dish, I guarantee everyone will love you. To make it easier, you can blanch the fries the day before, or prepare them to that stage on the day, several hours before they are needed.

SERVES 4

2 garlic cloves, crushed

1 tsp sea salt

1 tsp cayenne pepper, plus extra to season the fried chicken

½ tsp ground cumin

¼ tsp English mustard powder

½ tsp ground coriander

½ tsp sweet paprika

1 tsp onion powder

1 tsp cracked black pepper

2 tbsp chopped mixed thyme, rosemary and oregano

Dash of Tabasco sauce

4 x 175g (6oz) skinless, boneless chicken breasts

400ml (14fl oz/1¾ cups) buttermilk

175g (6oz/1¼ cups) plain (all-purpose) flour

3 tbsp cornflour (cornstarch)

Sunflower oil, for deep-frying

Sea salt and freshly ground black pepper

FOR THE SPICY FRIES

4 large floury (mealy) potatoes (such as Maris Piper or Desirée)

Sunflower oil, for deep-frying

1 tsp cayenne pepper

1 tsp paprika

Sea salt

FOR THE RANCH MAYO

150ml (5fl oz/⅔ cup) mayonnaise (homemade or ready-made)

2 tbsp sour cream

½ onion, grated

1 small garlic clove, crushed

1 tbsp chopped flat-leaf parsley

1 tsp snipped chives

Juice of ¼ lemon

A little Tabasco, to taste

The day before, make a marinade. Place the garlic and sea salt in a mortar and grind to a paste. Transfer to a large shallow dish and add half each of the cayenne pepper, cumin, mustard powder, coriander, paprika, onion powder and black pepper. Add the chopped herbs and Tabasco, and mix well.

Cut each chicken breast into 8 large chunks. Add to the marinade, cover with clingfilm (plastic wrap) and put in the fridge to marinate for 4 hours. Remove from the fridge and add the buttermilk. Mix well, cover again with clingfilm (plastic wrap) and return to the fridge to marinate overnight.

For the fries, peel the potatoes, rinse under cold water, then dry in a clean tea towel (dishtowel). Cut into pieces about 1cm (½in) x 5–7cm (2–2¾in).

Put the oil in a deep-fat fryer or in a large pan and heat to about 150°C (300°F). Blanch the potatoes in 2 batches for 5–8 minutes per batch until softened but still pale in colour. Remove to kitchen paper (paper towels) and set aside.

The next day, make the ranch mayo. In a bowl, mix together the mayonnaise, sour cream, onion, garlic, parsley, chives, lemon juice and Tabasco. Season with salt and pepper and set aside.

Combine the flour, cornflour (cornstarch), a little sea salt and the remaining cayenne pepper, cumin, mustard powder, coriander, paprika, onion powder and black pepper.

Remove the chicken pieces from the marinade with a slotted spoon and dip in the seasoned flour.

Heat the oil in a deep-fat fryer or large pan to 160–170°C (320–340°F). Carefully immerse the chicken in the hot oil and fry for 5–8 minutes, or until cooked and crisp. You may need to do this in batches.

Meanwhile, complete the spicy fries. Heat a fresh batch of oil to 200°C (400°F). Return the blanched fries to the oil for 2–3 minutes until golden and crisp.

Remove from the pan to kitchen paper (paper towels) to remove any excess oil. Season with the cayenne pepper, paprika and a good sprinkling of sea salt.

Remove the chicken onto kitchen paper (paper towels) to drain. Lightly season the fried chicken with sea salt and cayenne pepper. Serve with a generous spoonful of ranch mayo and with the spicy fries.

Crispy tamarind-fried quails *with spicy potatoes and coconut chutney*

Deep-frying meat such as quail or chicken is popular throughout Asia. Marinating the meat for two days beforehand develops sweet-and-sour overtones that are out of this world. I sometimes replace the quails with poussins. By the way, do not forget the crispy fried sediments from the marinade: I have sprinkled them over the meat as a garnish.

SERVES 4

8 quails, spatchcocked (see p.36)

Vegetable oil, for deep-frying

4 large Iceberg lettuce leaves, used as cups

Coriander (cilantro), chopped, to garnish

FOR THE MARINADE

3 garlic cloves, crushed

2 tsp ground coriander

1 red chilli, chopped

2 stalks of lemongrass, finely chopped

1 tsp ground turmeric

2 tbsp tamarind paste

1 tbsp light brown sugar

1 tsp garam masala

FOR THE CHUTNEY

125g (4½oz/generous 1⅓ cups) desiccated (dry unsweetened) coconut

2 green chillies, finely chopped

2.5cm (1in) piece of root ginger, peeled and finely chopped

2 tbsp chopped coriander (cilantro)

FOR THE SPICY POTATOES

4 tbsp peanut oil

1kg (2¼lb) small waxy new potatoes (such as Charlotte or Juliette), cooked and halved

250g (9oz) French (green) beans, cooked and halved

1 tbsp garam masala

1 tbsp chopped coriander (cilantro)

1 tbsp chopped mint

Juice of ½ lemon

250g (9oz) shallots, thinly sliced

Seeds of 1 large pomegranate

Sea salt and feshly ground black pepper

Start two days in advance by making the marinade. In a shallow dish, mix together the garlic, coriander, chilli, lemongrass, turmeric, tamarind paste, sugar and garam masala. Add the spatchcocked quails and coat with the marinade. Cover with clingfilm (plastic wrap) and put in the fridge to marinate for 48 hours.

On the day the dish is needed, prepare the spicy potatoes. Put 1 tbsp oil in a frying pan (skillet) over a medium heat. When the oil is hot, add the potatoes and French (green) beans. Fry for 10–12 minutes until lightly golden. Add the garam masala and cook for 1 minute. Add the coriander (cilantro) and mint and season with salt and pepper.

Transfer the mixture to a bowl and add the lemon juice and remaining oil. Leave to cool, then add the shallots and pomegranate seeds. Set aside.

For the chutney, in a bowl, mix together the coconut, chillies, ginger and coriander (cilantro). Set aside.

Place the quails and their marinade in a large shallow frying pan (skillet). Just cover the quails with water and bring to the boil. Reduce the heat and simmer for 5–6 minutes, or until the quails are cooked. Remove from the pan with a slotted spoon and set aside.

Continue to cook the sediments in the pan until all the water has evaporated. Remove the sediments and set aside.

Heat the oil to 170°C (325°F) in a deep-fat fryer. Carefully immerse the quails in the hot oil and fry for 3–4 minutes, or until cooked and crisp. You may need to do this in 2 batches. Remove with a slotted spoon onto kitchen paper (paper towels) to drain.

Add the sediments to the hot oil in the fryer and cook for 30 seconds to 1 minute until crispy. Remove with a slotted spoon onto kitchen paper (paper towels) to drain.

Divide the spicy potatoes between the Iceberg lettuce cups. Add some coconut chutney and garnish with chopped coriander (cilantro). Place the crispy fried quails alongside and scatter with the crispy fried sediments. Serve immediately.

BRAISING AND CASSEROLING

Braising and casseroling (the latter is often also known as stewing) are basically the same technique. You sear the food at a high temperature, then add a stock or sauce, cover the cooking pot and cook the food long and slow. Purists sometimes say that casseroling should be done on the hob, using heat from below, but these days many ovens offer you the possibility of cooking with bottom heat, so the distinctions are well and truly blurred. Whatever you call them, these cooking techniques produce poultry that is wonderfully soft, rich and meltingly tender. So who cares what names you use?

Squab pigeons with freekeh, hummus & herb oil

Egyptians have always loved eating meat, and squab pigeon is a particular favourite of theirs. It is often stuffed with rice or with cracked wheat, as in this recipe. Freekeh – cracked green wheat – is fast becoming the trendy new ingredient. Available from Middle Eastern stores and a supermarket near you very soon, it is tasty and extremely nutritious.

SERVES 4

275g (9½oz/generous 1 cup) freekeh

4 x 450g (1lb) squab pigeons with their giblets

175g (6oz) cleaned chicken livers

Juice of ½ lemon

25g (scant 1oz/1¾ tbsp) unsalted butter

1 onion, finely chopped

2 tsp ground cinnamon

½ tsp ground allspice

1 tbsp chopped flat-leaf parsley

75g (2½oz/½ cup) raisins, soaked in warm water for 30 minutes, then drained

2 tbsp chopped mint

900ml (1½ pints/4 cups) hot white chicken stock (see p.21)

Sea salt and freshly ground black pepper

50g (1¾oz/½ cup) flaked (slivered) almonds, toasted, to serve

300g (11oz/1¼ cups) hummus (homemade or bought), to serve

FOR THE HERB OIL

100ml (3½fl oz/scant ½ cup) olive oil

3 spring onions (scallions), finely chopped

2 tbsp chopped coriander (cilantro)

2 tbsp chopped mint

25g (scant 1oz/scant ¼ cup) pine nuts, toasted

Place the freekeh in a bowl, cover with water and leave to soak for 30 minutes.

Preheat the oven to 180°C (350°F/Gas 4).

Remove the giblets from the squab pigeons and cut into small dice. Ask your butcher to do this if you prefer. Dice the chicken livers. Set the giblets and livers aside.

Place the squab pigeons in a shallow dish, season liberally with salt and pepper and squeeze over the lemon juice. Set aside.

Heat the butter in a frying pan (skillet) over a medium heat. When the butter is hot, add the onion and cook for 2–3 minutes until lightly golden. Add the giblets, chicken livers, cinnamon and allspice. Cook for 2 minutes more.

Drain the freekeh thoroughly, then dry in a clean tea towel (dishtowel). Add to the pan together with the parsley, raisins and mint. Stir together well and season with salt and pepper. Leave to cool slightly.

Stuff a little freekeh into the cavity of each squab pigeon. Set aside the remainder.

Transfer the stuffed squab pigeons to a large lidded flameproof and ovenproof casserole dish (Dutch oven). Add the hot stock and bring to the boil.

Reduce the heat, cover with the lid and transfer to the preheated oven. Braise for 30 minutes, basting the squab pigeons once or twice with the cooking liquid.

Add the remaining freekeh to the dish. Cover with the lid again and return to the oven for 30 minutes more.

Remove from the oven and leave to rest for 5 minutes.

Meanwhile prepare the herb oil. Put the oil in a pan over a low heat. When the oil is hot, add the spring onions (scallions), coriander (cilantro) and mint. Cook, stirring, for 2–3 minutes.

Add the pine nuts and cook for 1 minute more. Transfer to a small blender or use a hand blender and blitz to a coarse purée.

To serve, divide the freekeh between the serving plates. Cut the squab pigeons into leg and breast portions and divide between the plates. Scatter with the almonds and drizzle with herb oil. Serve immediately, with the hummus alongside.

Chicken casserole *with orange blossom honey, tomato and chickpeas*

Orange blossom honey is a revelation. It gives a subtle hint of orange to this simple, hearty casserole – as well as being amazing when spread lavishly on toast or spooned over hot rice pudding. If you can't find it, use regular honey and add 100ml (3½fl oz/scant ½ cup) concentrated orange juice at the same time as you add the stock.

SERVES 4

4 x 175g (6oz) French-trim chicken breasts (see p.16)

½ tsp good-quality saffron strands

2 tbsp olive oil

1 onion, finely chopped

2 garlic cloves, crushed

2.5cm (1in) piece of root ginger, peeled and finely chopped

3 tbsp orange blossom honey

½ tsp ground cinnamon

800ml (28fl oz/3½ cups) white chicken stock (see p.21)

800g (1¾lb) ripe tomatoes, skinned and chopped or 1 x 400g (14oz) can chopped tomatoes in juice

2 tbsp chopped coriander (cilantro)

175g (6oz/scant 1¼ cups) cooked chickpeas

Sea salt and freshly ground black pepper

Preheat the oven to 180°C (350°F/Gas 4).

Season the chicken breasts with salt and pepper and rub with the saffron.

Place the oil in a shallow, lidded frying pan (skillet) over a medium heat. When the oil is hot, add the chicken breasts and fry for 2–3 minutes until golden. Remove from the pan with a slotted spoon and set aside.

Add the onion, garlic and ginger to the pan and cook for 1 minute.

Add the honey, cinnamon, stock and tomatoes. Bring to the boil. Return the chicken to the pan and cover with a lid. Reduce the heat and braise over a low heat for 12–15 minutes until the chicken is tender and cooked.

Remove the chicken to a plate with a slotted spoon. Cover with foil to keep warm.

Add the coriander (cilantro) and chickpeas to the pan. Heat through thoroughly and season with salt and pepper.

Divide the breasts between the serving plates and pour over the sauce. Serve immediately.

Preserved poultry (confit)

This method of preserving poultry was first developed by the farmers of south-west France to preserve the meat of the geese and ducks that they bred for their livers (*foie gras*). It's a simple technique that involves salting the meat and adding various aromatics such as garlic, bay leaves and thyme. The meat is then cooked very slowly to melting tenderness and, as it cooks, it renders its fat.

The resulting confit poultry can be used in many dishes: it's especially delicious with lentils and in salads. The rendered fat produced during the cooking is wonderful for roasting potatoes and root vegetables.

Here is my basic recipe. You can prepare any bird this way but the cooking time will vary according to the type of poultry. If you want, you can make your own duck fat to start you off, though it is now readily available in many supermarkets and delis.

MAKES 8 CONFIT LEGS
8 large duck legs, skin on
100g (3½oz/⅓ cup) sea salt

4 large heads of garlic, halved
2 small bay leaves
4 sprigs of thyme
3 litres (5¼ pints/2.6 quarts) duck fat

The day before, place the duck legs in a shallow dish that will hold all the legs in one layer. Add the salt, garlic, bay leaves and thyme. Mix together well.

Cover the dish with clingfilm (plastic wrap) and leave to marinate at room temperature for 1 day.

The next day, preheat the oven to 5°C (41°F) or to its lowest possible setting.

Remove the duck legs from the salt mix and brush off the excess salt. Rinse under cold running water and dry with a clean tea towel (dishtowel).

Put the duck fat in a large lidded flameproof and ovenproof casserole dish (Dutch oven) over a medium heat. When the fat has melted, add the duck legs.

Cover with a lid and cook in the preheated oven for 2½–3 hours, or until the legs are meltingly tender and the meat is almost falling off the bone.

Remove the legs with a slotted spoon and leave to cool slightly. Transfer to sterilised preserving jars. Pour over the warm duck fat to completely cover the legs. Leave to go cold and for the fat to solidify.

Seal the jars and refrigerate until ready to use.

Murgh makhna

This Mogul Indian speciality has a creamy, buttery taste, hence its English name, Indian butter chicken. I simply love it. I must be truthful: whenever I make this dish I serve it with plain basmati rice or toasted naan bread. Actually, to be really truthful, I serve it with both!

SERVES 4

1kg (2¼lb) boneless chicken thighs, cut into large pieces

1.8kg (4lb) ghee or clarified butter

1 onion, finely chopped

4 curry leaves

3 tbsp chopped coriander (cilantro), plus extra to garnish

75ml (2½fl oz/⅓ cup) double (heavy) cream , plus extra for drizzling

Sea salt

Cooked basmati rice and/or naan bread, toasted, to serve

FOR THE MARINADE

2.5cm (1in) piece of root ginger, peeled and finely chopped

2 large garlic cloves, crushed

100g (3½oz/⅔ cup) almonds, finely ground

150ml (5fl oz/⅔ cup) Greek-style natural yogurt

½ tsp red chilli powder

¼ tsp ground cloves

1 cinnamon stick

1 tsp garam masala

6 cardamom pods, crushed

1 x 400g (14oz) can chopped tomatoes in juice

The day before, make the marinade. Put the ginger and garlic in a mortar and crush to a paste.

Put the paste in a large dish with the almonds, yogurt, chilli powder, cloves, cinnamon stick, garam masala, cardamom, tomatoes and a little salt.

Add the chicken pieces and mix well. Cover with clingfilm (plastic wrap) and put in the fridge to marinate overnight.

The next day, preheat the oven to 180°C (350°F/Gas 4). Put the ghee in a shallow flameproof and ovenproof dish over a medium heat. When the ghee is hot, add the onion and curry leaves. Fry for 8–10 minutes until the onion is lightly golden.

Add the marinated chicken, increase the heat and fry for 2–3 minutes.

Add the coriander (cilantro) and cook for 1 minute more. Add the cream and gently mix with the chicken.

Transfer the dish to the preheated oven. Cook for 1–1¼ hours, or until the chicken is tender. If the top browns too quickly, cover the dish with a lid.

Just before serving, remove the lid, if using, and return the dish to the oven to brown the top. Alternatively, place the dish under a hot grill (broiler).

Drizzle with a little more double (heavy) cream and garnish with chopped coriander (cilantro). Serve immediately with basmati rice – and with toasted naan bread if you dare!

Braised duck *with figs, white balsamic vinegar and mint*

Duck legs are relatively cheap and they taste delicious. Slow-braising them produces a sauce with a wonderful flavour. White balsamic vinegar, although not yet as popular as the darker variety, is now becoming more easily sourced from good Italian delis. Tender butter-glazed baby turnips as a side are all you need to complete this dish.

SERVES 4

12 good-quality dried figs

200ml (7fl oz/scant 1 cup) port (any type will do)

4 large duck legs

1 tbsp plain (all-purpose) flour

4 tbsp sunflower oil

10g (¼oz/¾ tbsp) unsalted butter

2 tbsp chopped mint leaves, stalks reserved

25g (scant 1oz/2 tbsp) caster (superfine) sugar

75ml (2½fl oz/⅓ cup) white balsamic vinegar

800ml (28fl oz/3½ cups) brown chicken stock (see p.21)

Sea salt and freshly ground black pepper

The day before, put the figs in a bowl with the port. Cover with clingfilm (plastic wrap) and put in the fridge to marinate overnight.

The next day, preheat the oven to 170°C (325°F/Gas 3).

Season the duck legs with salt and pepper, then dip them in the flour. Shake of any excess flour.

Put the oil in a large lidded flameproof and ovenproof casserole dish (Dutch oven) over a medium heat. When the oil is hot, add the duck legs and cook for 5 minutes on each side until golden. Remove with a slotted spoon to a plate and set aside.

Pour off the excess oil from the casserole dish (Dutch oven) and reduce the heat. Add the butter, mint stalks, sugar and balsamic vinegar. Cook over a low heat for 4–5 minutes until lightly caramelised.

Return the duck legs to the casserole dish (Dutch oven).

Remove the figs from the port with a slotted spoon and pour the port over the duck legs. Add the chicken stock and bring to the boil.

Reduce the heat to a simmer and tuck in the marinated figs. Cover with a lid and transfer to the preheated oven.

Braise for 2–2½ hours, or until the duck is tender. Add a little more stock if it starts to dry out.

Carefully remove the duck legs and figs with a slotted spoon and divide between the serving plates. Strain the cooking sauce through a fine sieve (strainer) into a small pan and bring to the boil. Add the chopped mint leaves, pour over the duck legs and serve immediately.

Beer-braised chicken legs *with tobacco onions and avocado*

Chicken braised in beer is delicious. The beer gives it a slightly sweet taste and a unique flavour. The tobacco onions are extremely moreish, too. As well as being great with this dish, they also work well as a side dish for burgers. I could eat them all day long!

SERVES 4

4 chicken legs

2 tbsp plain (all-purpose) flour

2 tbsp sunflower oil

25g (scant 1oz/1¾ tbsp) unsalted butter

1 shallot, finely chopped

1 garlic clove, crushed

1 green serrano chilli, halved, deseeded and finely chopped

2 tsp ground cumin

1 tsp ground coriander

1 bottle Mexican-style beer (such as Corona)

1 x 400g (14oz) can chopped tomatoes in juice

1 tbsp chopped oregano

700ml (25floz/generous 3 cups) brown chicken stock (see p.21)

1 large avocado

Juice of ½ lime

Sea salt and freshly ground black pepper

Oregano leaves, to serve

FOR THE ONIONS

45g (1½oz/⅓ cup) plain (all-purpose) flour

2 tsp paprika

1 tsp sea salt

1 tsp cracked black pepper

1 tsp cayenne pepper

2 Spanish onions, cut into 5mm (¼in) slices

Sunflower oil, for deep-frying

Preheat the oven to 190°C (375°F/Gas 5).

Season the chicken legs with salt and pepper, then dip them in the flour.

Put the oil and butter in a lidded flameproof and ovenproof casserole dish (Dutch oven) over a medium heat. When they are hot, add the chicken legs and fry for 5–8 minutes, stirring occasionally, until golden all over.

Add the shallot, garlic, chilli, cumin and coriander. Cook for 2 minutes.

Add the beer, tomatoes, oregano and stock. Bring to the boil then reduce the heat to a simmer.

Cover the dish with a lid and put in the preheated oven. Braise for 45–50 minutes, basting once or twice as the chicken legs cook.

When the chicken is cooked and if the sauce is too thin, remove the chicken with a slotted spoon to a plate. Put the casserole dish (Dutch oven) over a medium heat and cook until the sauce thickens. Return the chicken to the dish and set aside, covered with the lid, to keep warm.

Cut the avocado in half and remove the stone and skin. Put the flesh in a blender with the lime juice and blitz to a smooth purée. Set aside.

Prepare the tobacco onions. In a bowl, combine the flour, paprika, salt, pepper and cayenne pepper. Toss the onions in the mixture to coat them. Set aside.

Put the oil in a deep pan or deep-fat fryer and heat to 180°C (350°F).

Remove the onions from the flour mixture and shake off any excess flour.

Fry the onions in the hot oil until crisp and dark golden brown. You may have to do this in batches.

Remove with a slotted spoon to kitchen paper (paper towels) to drain.

Place a chicken leg on each serving plate with some avocado purée alongside.

Pour the cooking sauce over the chicken and top with a generous pile of tobacco onions. Sprinkle with the oregano and serve immediately.

Goose daube *with orange, olives and rosemary*

A daube is traditionally cooked in a special deep earthenware dish called a *daubière*, but a regular casserole dish (Dutch oven) with a lid will do. The long, slow cooking produces a sauce with a rich, long-lasting flavour.

SERVES 6–8

1 x 4kg (8lb 13oz) goose, cut into leg and breast joints

4 tbsp sunflower oil

1 litre (1¾ pints/4 cups) brown chicken stock (see p.21)

20 plump black olives, pitted

2 large sprigs of rosemary

3 strips of orange peel

1 bouquet garni (1 bay leaf, sprig of thyme and 1 x 5cm (2in) piece of leek tied with kitchen string)

Sea salt and freshly ground black pepper

FOR THE MARINADE

2 onions, cut into large pieces

2 carrots, cut into 15mm (½in) cubes

375ml (13fl oz/1⅔ cups) good-quality red wine

3 strips of orange peel

2 garlic cloves, crushed

2 celery sticks, cut into 15mm (½in) cubes

2 small bay leaves

The day before, cut the goose leg joints into drumsticks and thighs. Remove the bones and cut the meat into 2.5cm (1in) dice. Cut the breast meat into 2.5cm (1in) dice.

Make the marinade. In a bowl, combine the onions, carrots, wine, orange peel, garlic, celery and bay leaves. Add the goose meat and mix together. Cover with clingfilm (plastic wrap) and put in the fridge to marinate overnight.

The next day, preheat the oven to 150°C (300°F/ Gas 2).

Remove the goose meat from the marinade with a slotted spoon and dry on a clean tea towel (dishtowel). Drain the marinade into a colander set over a bowl and reserve both the marinade and the contents of the colander.

Heat the oil in a large lidded flameproof and ovenproof casserole dish (Dutch oven) over a medium heat. When the oil is hot, add the goose meat.

Fry for 5–6 minutes until golden. Remove with a slotted spoon and set aside.

Put the onions, carrots, orange peel, garlic, celery and bay leaves drained from the marinade in the casserole dish (Dutch oven). Fry for 5 minutes until lightly golden.

Return the goose meat to the casserole dish (Dutch oven). Add the marinade and stock and bring to the boil. Add the olives, rosemary, 3 more strips of orange peel and the bouquet garni.

Cover with a lid and place in the preheated oven. Braise for 2–2½ hours until the goose is tender.

Remove the goose with a slotted spoon to a serving dish. Return the casserole dish (Dutch oven) to the hob and cook over a medium heat until the cooking liquid has reduced to a sauce with a syrupy consistency. Remove the bouquet garni and bay leaves, and season with salt and pepper. Pour the sauce over the goose and serve immediately.

Caneton a l'orange

A beautifully prepared duck in orange sauce is one of the greatest culinary treats in the French repertoire but it is a bit time-consuming to make, which may be why even restaurants hardly ever serve it nowadays. You have to prepare it in various stages: first pot-roasting the duck, then braising it in its wonderful caramelised orange sauce. My version is somewhat quicker, so give it a go. This dish is sometimes known as Caneton à la bigarade, as it was made using bitter Seville oranges – *bigarades*. I often serve my duck in orange sauce with buttered spinach and corn fritters (see p.120).

SERVES 4

1 duck (2–2.5kg (4½–5½lb), wings removed and set aside

2 tbsp sunflower oil

1 onion, cut into large chunks

2 carrots, cut into large chunks

50g (1¾oz/3½ tbsp) unsalted butter, softened

200ml (7fl oz/scant 1 cup) dry white wine

3 tbsp caster (superfine) sugar

75ml (2½fl oz/⅔ cup) red wine vinegar

Juice of 4 oranges

800ml (28fl oz/3½ cups) duck stock or brown chicken stock (see p.21)

2 tbsp orange liqueur (such as Curaçao or Grand Marnier)

2 oranges

1 tsp cornflour (cornstarch) (optional)

1 tbsp water (optional)

Sea salt and freshly ground black pepper

Preheat the oven to 180°C (350°F/Gas 4) and season the duck liberally with salt and pepper.

Heat the oil in a large lidded flameproof and ovenproof casserole dish (Dutch oven) over a medium heat.

When the oil is hot, add the duck. Fry for 6–8 minutes until golden all over. Remove with a slotted spoon and set aside.

Add the duck wings to the dish and fry for 5 minutes to colour them. Add the onion and carrots and fry for 5–6 minutes until browned. Return the duck to the dish, placing it on top of the wings and vegetables.

Smear the duck with the butter and add the wine. Cover with a lid, bring to the boil and boil for 3–4 minutes.

Transfer to the preheated oven and cook for 45 minutes. Remove the lid from the dish so the skin of the duck will brown, then return to the oven for 15–30 minutes more until the duck is cooked.

Meanwhile, make the base for the orange sauce. Place the sugar and vinegar in a pan over a low heat. When the sugar has dissolved, increase the heat and cook until it forms an amber-coloured caramel.

Immediately remove from the heat and add the orange juice. Take care as the caramel is extremely hot and will splatter.

Return the pan to the heat and add the stock and orange liqueur. Cook for 2–3 minutes, then remove from the heat. Set this orange sauce base aside.

Remove the zest from the 2 oranges, then peel the oranges and separate the segments. Set the segments aside.

Blanch the zest in a small pan of boiling water for 2–3 minutes, then drain it well. Set aside.

Carefully remove the cooked duck from the casserole dish (Dutch oven) onto a large chopping (cutting) board. Leave to cool slightly, then cut into 8 joints (see p.26).

Strain the cooking juices from the dish into a small pan and bring to the boil. Skim off any fat that rises to the surface using a small knife.

Add the orange sauce base. If the sauce is too thin, mix the cornflour (cornstarch) with the water and whisk this into the boiling sauce. Boil for 1 minute.

Return the duck joints to the dish and add the orange sauce. Add the orange zest, cover with the lid and return to the oven for 25 minutes more.

Divide the duck and orange sauce between the serving plates. Top with the orange segments and serve immediately.

Chicken drumsticks
with borlotti beans, tuscan sausage and black chickpeas

For this recipe I suggest using Tuscan sausages made with garlic and fennel seeds. Black chickpeas – *ceci neri* – should be available from Italian delis.

SERVES 4

300g (11oz/1¾ cups) dried borlotti beans

200g (7oz/generous 1 cup) Italian black chickpeas (ceci neri)

2 litres (3½ pints/8 cups) water

2 tbsp olive oil

12 chicken drumsticks

12 garlic cloves, whole

4 Tuscan sausages, cut into 1cm (½in) slices

750ml (1¼ pints/3⅔ cups) brown chicken stock (see p.21)

15g (½oz/1 tbsp) unsalted butter, chilled and cut into small pieces

2 tbsp chopped flat-leaf parsley

Sea salt and freshly ground black pepper

The day before, put the beans and chickpeas in separate bowls, covered with cold water. Leave to soak overnight.

The next day, drain the beans and chickpeas and put in separate pans. Cover each with 1 litre (1¾ pints/ 4 cups) cold water and bring to the boil. Reduce the heat and simmer for about 45 minutes until both are cooked. Drain well.

Put the oil in a large pan over a medium heat. When the oil is hot, add the chicken drumsticks and fry for 8–10 minutes until golden all over.

Add the garlic and sausages and cook for 4–5 minutes until both are lightly golden.

Add the stock and bring to the boil. Reduce the heat, then add the drained beans and chickpeas.

Cover with a lid and cook for 20–25 minutes until the drumsticks are cooked through and tender.

Season with salt and pepper. Add the butter and parsley, stir well and serve immediately.

Coq au mâcon rouge

Coq au vin is perhaps the most famous classic French dish. It's been travelling around the world for years. Although a classic, it consists of nothing more than chicken braised in red wine. Traditionally, it was made using a cock bird and the sauce was thickened with the bird's own blood. Some people, including myself, think it's a pity that this practice has all but died out. Any good-quality red wine will make a great base for the sauce, but I use a Mâcon. I always buy two bottles – one for the sauce and one to drink. I recommend some buttery mash potatoes as an accompaniment. Bon appétit and bonne santé!

SERVES 4

1 x 1.5–2kg (3lb 3oz–4½lb) chicken, cut into 8 joints (see pp.14–15)

2 tbsp sunflower oil

200g (7oz) piece of green bacon, rind removed and cut into 1cm (½in) cubes

300g (11oz/generous 3 cups) button (white) mushrooms, halved

200g (7oz) button onions, peeled

2 garlic cloves, crushed

1 small bay leaf

Small sprig of thyme

375ml (13fl oz/1⅔ cups) good-quality red wine (such as Mâcon)

150ml (5fl oz/⅔ cup) port (any type will do)

1 tbsp soft unsalted butter, mixed into a paste with 1 tbsp plain (all-purpose) flour

1 tbsp chopped flat-leaf parsley (optional)

Sea salt and freshly ground black pepper

Season the chicken joints with salt and pepper. Put the oil in a large lidded flameproof and ovenproof casserole dish (Dutch oven) over a medium heat. When the oil is hot, add the chicken and fry for 5–6 minutes until golden all over. You may need to do this in batches. Remove with a slotted spoon and set aside.

Add the bacon, mushrooms and onions to the dish. Fry for 5–8 minutes until golden.

Add the garlic, bay leaf and thyme, and mix well, then add the chicken pieces.

Pour over the wine and port, and cover with a tight-fitting lid. Bring to the boil, then reduce the heat and either simmer gently on the stove top for 45–60 minutes until the chicken is tender, or cook for the same amount of time in an oven preheated to 190°C (375°F/Gas 5).

When the chicken is cooked, remove the chicken and onions with a slotted spoon to a serving dish. Discard the bay leaf and thyme. Cover the serving dish with foil to keep warm.

Put the cassserole dish over a medium heat and bring the cooking sauce back to the boil. Whisk in the butter and flour mixture, a little at a time, to thicken the sauce. Cook for 2–3 minutes, then strain through a fine sieve (strainer). The sauce should coat the back of a spoon.

Pour the sauce over the chicken, add the button onions, and sprinkle with the parsley, if using. Serve immediately.

Normandy cider braised chicken

Normandy is famous for its apples, so in that region of France, they often cook chicken in their local cider. In Alsace, the same dish is prepared using Riesling wine. I think this dish is delicious served with buttered noodles, as here, but purists like it served with mashed potatoes.

SERVES 4

4 large chicken legs cut into thigh and drumstick portions (see pp.14–15)

2 tbsp sunflower oil

30g (1oz/2 tbsp) unsalted butter

4 large shallots, finely chopped

2 Cox apples

300ml (10fl oz/1¼ cups) dry cider (preferably Normandy cider)

100ml (3½fl oz/scant ½ cup) white chicken stock (see p.21)

75ml (2½fl oz/⅓ cup) double (heavy) cream or crème fraîche

Sea salt and freshly ground black pepper

Buttered noodles, to serve

Season the chicken portions with salt and pepper.

Put the oil and butter in a large lidded frying pan (skillet) over a medium heat. When they are hot, add the chicken and fry for 4–5 minutes on each side until browned.

Pour off the excess cooking fat and add the shallots. Cover with a lid and sweat for 2 minutes.

Peel and core the apples and cut into small wedges.

Add the cider and stock to the pan. Bring to the boil, then reduce the heat and add the apple.

Cover with the lid and braise for 15 minutes, or until the chicken is cooked through.

Remove the chicken and apple from the pan with a slotted spoon and transfer to a dish. Cover with foil to keep warm.

Return the pan to the heat, add the cream and bring to the boil. Reduce the heat and return the chicken and apple to the pan. Simmer for 5 minutes, then season with salt and pepper. Divide between the serving plates and pour over the sauce. Serve immediately with buttered noodles.

Fesenjan duck *in pomegranate and walnut sauce*

Fesenjan – a Persian stew – is often served on special occasions. Although traditionally made with duck, as here, or game, such as squab pigeon or pheasant, it is equally good made with chicken. The sauce should be thick and its flavour full of sweet-and-sour overtones. If pomegranate molasses are not available, use the same amount of pomegranate juice instead.

SERVES 4

2 tbsp olive oil

25g (scant 1oz/1¾ tbsp) unsalted butter

1 duck, approx 2.5kg (5½lb), cut into breast and leg portions

2 onions, thinly sliced

60g (2oz/scant ⅓ cup) caster (superfine) sugar

1 tsp ground cinnamon

Pinch of ground turmeric

300g (11oz/3 cups) shelled walnuts

450ml (15fl oz/2 cups) white chicken stock (see p.21)

60ml (2fl oz/¼ cup) pomegranate molasses

Juice of 2 lemons

Seeds of 1 large pomegranate

Freshly cooked rice, to serve

Put the oil and butter in a large flameproof casserole dish (Dutch oven) over a medium heat. When they are hot, add the duck portions and fry for 5–8 minutes until golden all over. Remove with a slotted spoon to a dish and set aside.

Add the onions and sugar to the casserole dish (Dutch oven) and fry for 4–5 minutes until the onions are lightly caramelised.

Reduce the heat and add the cinnamon and turmeric. Cook over a low heat for 1 minute. Return the duck to the casserole dish (Dutch oven).

Place 100g (3½oz/1 cup) walnuts in a food processor and blitz to a fine powder. Stir these into the casserole dish (Dutch oven) and add the stock. Bring to the boil.

Reduce the heat and add the pomegranate molasses and lemon juice. Simmer for 1–1¼ hours, or until the duck is cooked and tender.

Just before serving, add the remaining walnuts and the pomegranate seeds. Serve immediately with freshly cooked rice.

Civet of poultry *with winter fruits and green peppercorns*

A civet is a slow-cooked stew of game or poultry. The meat is cooked in a rich wine-based sauce and the dish is usually finished with the blood of the meat used. You can make it with any kind of poultry – duck, chicken or guinea fowl. I couldn't decide which, so I decided to use a mixture. One beauty of this dish is that it can be prepared a day ahead and slowly reheated when needed.

SERVES 4

4 duck thighs

4 chicken thighs

4 squab pigeon breasts

2 tbsp plain (all-purpose) flour

2 tbsp sunflower oil

25g (scant 1oz/1¾ tbsp) unsalted butter

1 Granny Smith apple

12 prunes, pitted

2 tsp green peppercorns in brine, rinsed and drained

Sea salt and freshly ground black pepper

FOR THE MARINADE

1 carrot, chopped

1 onion, chopped

1 celery stick, chopped

600ml (1 pint/2½ cups) full-bodied red wine

2 sprigs of thyme

1 strip of orange peel

4 juniper berries

1 small bay leaf

6 black peppercorns

The day before, make the marinade. Put the carrot, onion, celery, wine, thyme, orange peel, juniper berries, bay leaf and black peppercorns in a deep dish. Add the poultry thighs and breasts. Cover with clingfilm (plastic wrap) and put in the fridge to marinate overnight.

The next day, drain in a colander set over a bowl. Set the marinade aside.

Dust the poultry pieces with flour and shake off any excess.

Put the oil and butter in a flameproof casserole dish (Dutch oven) over a medium heat. When they are hot, add the poultry pieces and fry for 5–6 minutes until golden all over.

Remove with a slotted spoon to a plate and set aside.

Add the carrot, onion and celery that were drained from the marinade to the casserole dish (Dutch oven). Fry for 5 minutes until golden brown.

Stir in the wine, thyme, orange peel and peppercorns from the marinade.

Reduce the heat and return the poultry pieces to the casserole dish (Dutch oven). Cover with a lid and simmer for 45–60 minutes, or until the meat is cooked and tender.

Remove the poultry pieces with a slotted spoon to a serving dish. Cover with foil to keep warm.

Strain the sauce through a fine sieve (strainer) into a clean pan. Peel and core the apple, and cut into 1cm (½in) cubes.

Add the apple, prunes and green peppercorns to the casserole dish (Dutch oven). Bring to the boil and boil for 1 minute. Season with salt and pepper.

Divide the poultry pieces between the serving dishes, pour over the sauce and serve immediately.

Guinea fowl casserole *with winter roots, pearl barley and parsley pistou*

If ever there was a winter-warming dish, then this is it. Accompanied by buttered new potatoes, it makes an ideal family meal. I have suggested making it with baby carrots and button onions, but it is also delicious with other winter vegetables, such as swede and parsnips. The parsley pistou adds a contrasting flavour of the Mediterranean.

SERVES 4

2 tbsp olive oil

1 guinea fowl, approx 1.5kg (3lb 3oz), cut into joints (see pp.14–15)

200g (7oz) baby button onions, peeled

1 garlic clove, crushed

75g (2½oz/⅓ cup) pearl barley

250ml (8fl oz/1 cup) dry white wine

600ml (1 pint/2½ cups) brown chicken stock (see p.21)

1 bay leaf

2 sprigs of thyme

2 sprigs of rosemary

150g (5½oz) baby carrots

Sea salt and freshly ground black pepper

FOR THE PISTOU

50g (1¾oz/1⅔ cups) flat-leaf parsley

3 tbsp olive oil

1 garlic clove

2 tbsp ground almonds

Heat 2 tbsp oil in a large, lidded flameproof casserole dish (Dutch oven) over a medium heat. When the oil is hot, add the guinea fowl joints and fry for 10–12 minutes until golden.

Add the onions and cook for 8–10 minutes until lightly golden. Add the garlic and pearl barley and mix well together.

Add the wine, bring to the boil and boil for 2–3 minutes. Add the stock and reduce the heat. Tuck in the bay leaf, thyme and rosemary. Cover with a lid and simmer gently for 25 minutes.

Add the carrots and cook for 20 minutes more.

Meanwhile, prepare the pistou. Place the parsley, oil, garlic and almonds in a small blender and blitz to a coarse pulp. Season with salt and pepper.

Season the casserole with salt and pepper, then divide between the serving bowls. Top each bowl with a spoonful of pistou and serve immediately.

Indonesian duck curry *with grapes and tomatoes, and kaffir lime*

This duck curry is an adaptation of a memorable duck curry that I ate in Asia during a holiday visit. I have to admit that my recipe has evolved over time. This is the latest version. The curry should taste tangy, salty and sweet, but the sourness of the lime juice should be the lead flavour.

SERVES 4

4 tbsp sunflower oil

2 tbsp sambal oelek (Indonesian red chilli paste)

4 roasted duck breasts, cut into 1cm (½in) slices

400ml (14fl oz/1¾ cups) coconut milk

300g (11oz/2 cups) seedless white grapes

200g (7oz/1⅓ cups) red cherry tomatoes

1 tbsp palm sugar or brown sugar

1 small red pepper (bell pepper), halved, deseeded and cut into strips

1 small yellow pepper (bell pepper), halved, deseeded and cut into strips

1 small green pepper (bell pepper), halved, deseeded and cut into strips

8 kaffir lime leaves, finely shredded

75ml (2½fl oz/⅔ cup) lime juice

10 Thai basil leaves

Sea salt

Freshly cooked steamed jasmine rice, to serve

Heat a wok or large frying pan (skillet) over a medium heat. When it is hot, add the oil and sambal oelek and fry for 2 minutes, stirring all the time, until the mixture becomes fragrant.

Add the sliced duck and cook for 1 minute, then add the coconut milk.

Bring to the boil, then add the grapes, tomatoes and palm sugar. Season with a little salt.

Add the red, yellow and green peppers (bell peppers), the kaffir lime leaves and the lime juice. Reduce the heat and simmer for 5 minutes until the peppers are soft and tender.

Add the Thai basil, remove from the heat and serve immediately, accompanied by steamed jasmine rice.

POACHING, SMOKING AND STEAMING

These techniques may not be the first that spring to mind when you are thinking of cooking poultry, but believe me, the results are tasty. To poach your poultry, you totally submerge it in liquid – usually water, wine or stock, but sometimes oil – and cook it for varying lengths of time, depending on the type of poultry and the size of the pieces. Smoking involves exposing it to smoke – mainly wood smoke. The poultry takes on a smoky flavour that is subtle and delicate. In steaming, you cook over boiling water or stock. The steam rises, envelops the food and cooks it quickly, at a high temperature, so it remains wonderfully moist and tender. You should definitely give these unusual techniques a go.

My chicken cotriade

This is my take on the classic Normandy cotriade, a dish that is traditionally made with local coastal fish, such as monkfish, hake and eel, along with a selection of shellfish like mussels and prawns (shrimp). In my version, I use shellfish combined with chicken, which I think works rather well.

SERVES 4

15g (½oz/1 tbsp) unsalted butter

1 garlic clove, crushed

2 carrots, cut into 15mm (½in) slices

2 onions, thinly sliced

Good pinch of saffron strands

200ml (7fl oz/scant 1 cup) Muscadet or other dry white wine

750ml (1¼ pints/3⅓ cups) white chicken stock (see p.21)

1 x 400g (14oz) can chopped tomatoes in juice

2 sprigs of thyme

500g (1lb 2oz) large new waxy potatoes (such as Charlotte)

4 x 150g (5½oz) skinless, boneless chicken breasts, cut into large cubes

375g (13oz) live mussels in their shells, scrubbed and de-bearded

300g (11oz) langoustines or king prawns (shrimp), peeled

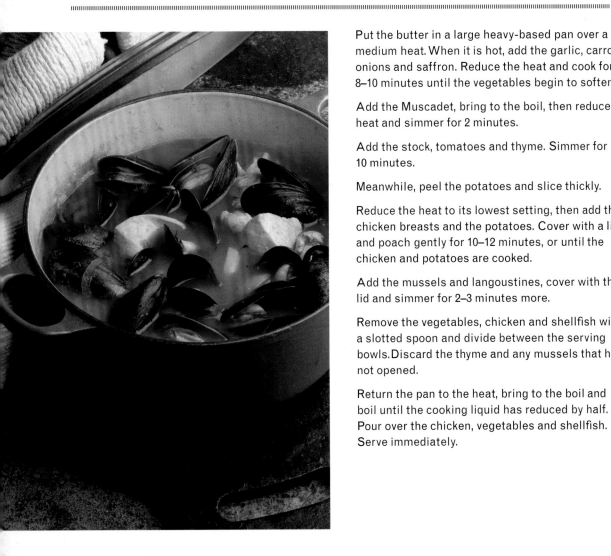

Put the butter in a large heavy-based pan over a medium heat. When it is hot, add the garlic, carrots, onions and saffron. Reduce the heat and cook for 8–10 minutes until the vegetables begin to soften.

Add the Muscadet, bring to the boil, then reduce the heat and simmer for 2 minutes.

Add the stock, tomatoes and thyme. Simmer for 10 minutes.

Meanwhile, peel the potatoes and slice thickly.

Reduce the heat to its lowest setting, then add the chicken breasts and the potatoes. Cover with a lid and poach gently for 10–12 minutes, or until the chicken and potatoes are cooked.

Add the mussels and langoustines, cover with the lid and simmer for 2–3 minutes more.

Remove the vegetables, chicken and shellfish with a slotted spoon and divide between the serving bowls. Discard the thyme and any mussels that have not opened.

Return the pan to the heat, bring to the boil and boil until the cooking liquid has reduced by half. Pour over the chicken, vegetables and shellfish. Serve immediately.

Chicken kabsa

Kabsa is the national dish of Saudi Arabia. Here I make it with chicken, which is first gently poached in a sweet, aromatic tomato broth that is then used to cook the rice. Dried limes (*loomi*) are available from Middle Eastern stores. It is worth trying to find them as they really do add an interesting flavour to the dish. Baharat spices are often known as Arabic seven spice blend. They are used a lot in Turkish and Middle Eastern cooking, and are especially good with lamb, but also with fish and vegetables – and with chicken, as this recipe proves!

SERVES 4

700g (1½lb) skinless, boneless chicken thighs, cut into large pieces

50g (1¾oz/3½ tbsp) unsalted butter

1 onion, thinly sliced

½ tsp ground cumin

½ tsp ground coriander

1 cinnamon stick

6 cardamom pods, cracked

½ tsp ground turmeric

½ tsp ground cloves

2 tsp baharat spices

1 tbsp tomato purée (paste)

2 dried limes

2 medium carrots, thickly sliced

1 courgette (zucchini), thickly sliced

½ red pepper (bell pepper), halved, deseeded and cut into thick strips

½ green pepper (bell pepper), halved, deseeded and cut into thick strips

800ml (28fl oz/3½ cups) water

200g (7oz/1 cup) basmati rice, rinsed under cold running water until the water runs clear, then drained

Sea salt and freshly ground black pepper

2 tbsp chopped flat-leaf parsley, to serve

Wedges of lemon, to garnish

Season the chicken pieces with salt and pepper. Put the butter in a large pan over a medium heat. When the butter is hot, add the chicken and fry for 5–6 minutes until lightly coloured.

Add the onion, cumin, coriander, cinnamon stick, cardamom pods, turmeric, cloves and baharat spices. Mix well.

Add the tomato purée (paste) and the dried limes. Cook for 2–3 minutes.

Add the carrots, courgette (zucchini) and the red and green (bell) peppers. Stir to combine.

Add the water and bring to the boil.

Reduce the heat and poach for 15–20 minutes, or until the chicken and vegetables are cooked. Remove the chicken and vegetables with a slotted spoon to a dish and cover with foil to keep warm.

Add the rice to the pan and mix well. Cover with a lid and cook over a low heat for 15–18 minutes until the rice is cooked.

Return the chicken and vegetables to the pan, and mix together carefully. Cover with the lid and steam for 5 minutes over a low heat.

Remove the cinnamon stick and the limes. Pack the mixture tightly into 4 bowls then unmould onto the serving plates. Sprinkle with parsley and garnish with wedges of lemon. Serve immediately.

Jamaican-style chicken *with apricot, cinnamon and star anise*

In this dish the chicken legs are steam-cooked in a fruit-tea broth, together with sweet apricots and spices. The result is extremely light and very delicious. My recipe also includes fried limes: frying them really accentuates their lovely flavour. I like to serve this dish with its hint of the Caribbean accompanied by some plain rice and a salad.

SERVES 4

4 chicken legs

3 tbsp olive oil

2 onions, thinly sliced

75ml (2½fl oz/scant ¼ cup) clear honey

4 star anise

2 cinnamon sticks

150ml (5fl oz/⅔ cup) prepared orange tea (2 tsp bought orange tea mixed with 300ml (10fl oz/ 1¼ cups) boiling water or 300ml (10fl oz/1¼ cups) prepared black tea with 1 tsp grated orange zest, left to steep for 5 minutes, then strained)

250ml (8fl oz/1 cup) white chicken stock (see p.21)

75g (2½oz/scant ½ cup) dried apricots, soaked in warm water for 30 minutes, then drained

2 small limes, halved

Sea salt and freshly ground black pepper

1 tbsp chopped coriander (cilantro), to serve

Season the chicken legs with salt and pepper. Put 2 tbsp oil in a lidded flameproof casserole dish (Dutch oven) over a medium heat. When the oil is hot, add the chicken legs. Fry for 5–6 minutes on each side until golden, then remove to a plate with a slotted spoon and set aside.

Add the onions to the casserole dish (Dutch oven) and fry for 5 minutes until golden. Add the honey and cook for 5 minutes until the onions are lightly caramelised.

Add the star anise and cinnamon sticks, followed by the prepared tea and the stock. Bring to the boil.

Return the chicken legs to the dish. Add the apricots, reduce the heat and cover with a lid. Cook for 40 minutes until the chicken is tender.

Meanwhile, heat a small frying pan (skillet) over a medium heat. When it is hot, add the remaining oil and the lime halves, cut side down. Cook for a few minutes until lightly golden.

Five minutes before the end of the cooking time, add the fried limes to the casserole dish (Dutch oven). Season with salt and pepper.

Remove the star anise and cinnamon sticks, Divide the chicken and apricots between the serving dishes and sprinkle with the chopped coriander (cilantro). Serve immediately.

Chicken and tuna salad *with a curry dressing*

This light salad is made using a combination of cold poached chicken and tuna, mixed together in a Thai-style curry dressing.

SERVES 4

900ml (1½ pints/4 cups) white chicken stock (see p.21)

4 x 150g (5½oz) skinless, boneless chicken breasts

1 carrot, cut into matchsticks

100g (3½oz) French (green) beans, cooked and halved

500g (1lb 2oz/5 cups) beansprouts, trimmed

1 x 100g (3½oz) can good-quality tuna in brine, drained

2 shallots, thinly sliced

200g (7oz) continental salad leaves

Sesame seeds, to serve

FOR THE DRESSING

2 tbsp vegetable oil

1 tbsp red curry paste

75ml (2½fl oz/⅓ cup) coconut milk

1 tbsp fish sauce (nam pla)

3 tbsp palm sugar

1 tbsp tamarind paste

Put the stock in a large pan and bring to the boil. Reduce the heat, then add the chicken breasts. Poach for 8–10 minutes until cooked through and tender.

Remove with a slotted spoon to a plate and leave until cool enough to handle. Shred the chicken and set aside.

Prepare the dressing. Put the oil in a wok over a high heat. When the oil is hot, add the curry paste and cook for 10 seconds, stirring all the time.

Add the coconut milk, fish sauce, palm sugar and tamarind paste. Cook for 2–3 minutes, still over a high heat, then transfer to a bowl and leave to go cold.

Meanwhile, put the carrot, French (green) beans, beansprouts, shredded chicken, tuna, shallots and salad leaves in a large bowl. Add the cooled dressing and toss well.

Divide between the serving bowls and sprinkle with sesame seeds. Serve immediately.

Poached guinea fowl *with tarragon, morels, muscat grapes*

If not cooked with care, guinea fowl can be a little on the dry side, but when it is poached or steamed, it is unfailingly juicy. Fresh morels, when in season in early spring, are fantastic, but during the rest of the year, dried morels make a great substitute.

SERVES 4

4 x 175g (6oz) French-trim skinless, boneless guinea fowl breasts (see p.16)

15g (½oz/1 tbsp) unsalted butter

3 tbsp dry white wine

100ml (3½fl oz/scant ½ cup) grape juice

400ml (14fl oz/1¾ cups) white chicken stock (see p.21)

150ml (5fl oz/⅔ cup) double (heavy) cream

175g (6oz/2⅔ cups) fresh morels, thoroughly washed and dried or 50g (1¾oz) dried morels, reconstituted in water for 30 minutes, then drained and dried

2 tbsp chopped tarragon

200g (7oz/1⅓ cups) Muscat grapes

Sea salt and freshly ground black pepper

Season the guinea fowl breasts with salt and pepper. Put the butter in a shallow pan over a medium heat. When the butter is hot, add the guinea fowl breasts and seal for 1 minute on each side, making sure that they do not colour.

Add the wine and grape juice and bring to the boil. Add the stock and cream, making sure that the breasts are immersed in the liquid. Reduce the heat and poach gently for 8–10 minutes.

Remove the breasts with a slotted spoon to a plate and cover with foil to keep warm.

Add the morels to the pan, increase the heat and cook for 10–12 minutes until the sauce has reduced and begins to coat the back of a spoon.

Add the tarragon and grapes, then return the breasts to the sauce for 2 minutes. Season with salt and pepper. Divide between the serving dishes and serve immediately.

Olive-oil poached chicken
with tapenade and summer aïoli vegetables

Poaching meat or fish in a warm bath of light olive oil keeps the food extremely moist and succulent. It is important to keep the temperature of the oil constant during the cooking. This poached chicken is delicious served warm or at room temperature.

SERVES 4

400–600ml (14fl oz–1 pint/1¾–2½ cups) light olive oil, plus 2 tbsp for the vegetables

1 head of garlic, halved widthways

4 x 175g (6oz) French-trim skinless chicken breasts (see p.16)

4 free-range eggs

175g (6oz) French (green) beans, cooked

8 asparagus tips, cooked

12 long red radishes, trimmed

1 x 200g (7oz) can chickpeas, rinsed and drained

8 red cherry tomatoes

8 yellow cherry tomatoes

Juice of ½ lemon

Sea salt and freshly ground black pepper

FOR THE TAPENADE

75g (2½oz/scant ½ cup) pitted black olives

1 garlic clove, crushed

2 anchovy fillets in oil, rinsed, drained and chopped

1 tbsp chopped flat-leaf parsley

4 tbsp olive oil

TO SERVE

Rocket (arugula)

Wedges of lemon

120ml (4fl oz/½ cup) garlic mayonnaise (aïoli: bought or homemade)

Put the oil in a small flameproof casserole dish (Dutch oven) over a low heat. Add the garlic and cook for 15 minutes until the oil reaches 93°C (200°F).

Add the chicken breasts, submerging them completely in the warm oil. Keeping the oil at a constant temperature, poach the breasts for 30 minutes until cooked through and tender.

Remove with a slotted spoon to kitchen paper (paper towels) to drain. Season with salt and set aside.

Meanwhile make the tapenade. Place the olives, garlic, anchovy fillets, parsley and oil in a small blender and blitz to a coarse paste. Season with a little salt and pepper to taste and set aside.

Bring a small pan of water to the boil and carefully add the eggs. Cook gently for 5 minutes until soft-boiled, then refresh under cold water and peel. Set aside.

Put the cooked French (green) beans and asparagus in a bowl with the radishes, chickpeas and red and yellow cherry tomatoes. Add the lemon juice and the 2 tbsp olive oil. Season with salt and pepper.

Divide the chicken breasts and vegetables between the serving plates or place on a serving platter. Spoon a little tapenade over each breast. Cut the soft-boiled eggs in half and divide between the plates.

Sprinkle over a few rocket (arugula) leaves and garnish with lemon wedges. Serve immediately accompanied by the garlic mayonnaise.

Asian-inspired pot-au-feu

Pot-au-feu – literally 'pot on the fire' – consists of chunks of meat and vegetables simmered for hours in a tasty broth. Since Asians, and especially the Chinese, are famous for their fragrant broths, the idea came to me to create this Asian-inspired pot-au-feu. It is simple and delicious, and most certainly a dish to enjoy on a cold winter's night.

SERVES 4

1.5kg (3lb 3oz) chicken, cut into 8 joints (see pp.14–15)

1 litre (1¾ pints/4 cups) white chicken stock (see p.21)

4cm (1½in) piece of root ginger, peeled and thinly sliced

2 carrots, thinly sliced

8 spring onions (scallions), cut into 2.5cm (1in) lengths

60ml (2fl oz/¼ cup) Shaoxing rice wine

2 stalks of lemongrass, finely chopped

4 star anise

1 x 400g (14oz) can water chestnuts, rinsed, drained and sliced

50g (1¾oz) dried Chinese black mushrooms, soaked in warm water for 1 hour, then drained and shredded

1 tbsp ketchup manis (Indonesian sweet soy sauce)

1 tbsp fish sauce (nam pla)

1 large skinless duck breast

100g (3½oz/3⅓ cups) baby spinach

50g (1¾oz/1⅔ cups) coriander (cilantro) leaves

Bring a large pan of water to the boil and add the chicken joints. Poach for 5 minutes, then drain.

Place the chicken joints in a clean, large, deep pan. Add the stock and bring to the boil.

Add the ginger, carrots, spring onions (scallions), rice wine, lemongrass, star anise, water chestnuts, mushrooms, ketchup manis and fish sauce.

Bring back to the boil, then reduce the heat. Poach for 40 minutes.

Add the duck breast and poach for 25 minutes more.

Remove the duck breast with a slotted spoon, slice thinly, then return it to the broth.

Add the spinach and the coriander (cilantro) and cook for 1 minute. Divide between 4 individual serving bowls and serve immediately.

Wok-smoked chicken *with wakami seaweed and mushroom broth*

I love the flavour obtained by smoking the chicken over tea in this recipe. The tea gives off a delicate, smoky aroma that permeates the chicken. The mushroom and seaweed-infused broth is the perfect medium for the smoked chicken – light and extremely flavoursome.

SERVES 4

4 x 175g (6oz) French-trim skinless chicken breasts (see p.16)

50g (1¾oz/¼ cup) basmati rice, or other rice of your choice

3 tbsp demerara (raw brown) sugar

50g (1¾oz) black tea leaves

FOR THE MARINADE

2 tbsp chopped coriander (cilantro)

1 tbsp sunflower oil, plus extra for greasing

1 tbsp shoyu (Japanese soy sauce)

2cm (¾in) piece of root ginger, peeled and grated

½ tsp sea salt

1 tsp caster (superfine) sugar

1 tsp ground star anise

FOR THE BROTH

600ml (1 pint/2½ cups) white chicken stock (see p.21)

6 shiitake mushrooms, trimmed and sliced

50g (1¾oz) dried wakami seaweed, soaked in warm water for 30 minutes, then drained

4 baby bok choy, cut into large pieces

50g (1¾oz) baby spinach leaves

1 tbsp white miso paste

1cm (½in) piece of root ginger, peeled and thinly sliced

For the marinade, put the coriander (cilantro), oil, shoyu, ginger, salt, caster (superfine) sugar and star anise in a large shallow dish. Add the chicken breasts and rub them all over with mixture.

Leave to marinate at room temperature for 1 hour.

Place a large piece of foil inside the wok and put the rice, demerara (raw brown) sugar and tea leaves in the bottom. Grease a rack that fits on top of the wok with a little oil to stop the breasts from sticking. Place the rack on top of the wok, over the smoking mixture.

Remove the chicken breasts from the marinade with a slotted spoon.

Slowly heat the wok and when the mixture begins to smoke, place the chicken breasts on the rack. Cover with a lid, reduce the heat to the lowest setting and smoke for 30 minutes.

Meanwhile, prepare the broth. Put the stock in a pan and bring to the boil. Add the mushrooms, seaweed, bok choy, spinach, miso paste and ginger. Reduce the heat and simmer for 10–12 minutes.

When the chicken breasts are ready, remove from the wok and transfer to a plate. Cover with foil and leave to rest for 5 minutes.

Divide the chicken breasts between the serving bowls and add the broth. Serve immediately.

Chicken legs steamed *in north african spices*

Steaming is a popular method of cooking in the countries of the Mahgreb – western north Africa – so here I've paid homage to this tradition by rubbing the chicken with North African spices before steaming it. Serve with couscous – to continue the North African theme – and a salad.

SERVES 4

1 tsp saffron strands

75g (2½oz/5 tbsp) unsalted butter

1 tbsp harissa paste

½ tsp ground coriander

½ tsp ground cumin

Good pinch of cayenne pepper

1 tsp ground turmeric

4 large chicken legs

Sea salt and freshly ground black pepper

Put the saffron in a mortar with 1 tsp salt and pound to a fine powder. Transfer to a bowl.

Put the butter in a pan over a medium heat. When it has just melted, add the powdered saffron.

Add the harissa, coriander, cumin, cayenne pepper, turmeric and black pepper.

Score the chicken legs to the bone at intervals with a sharp knife and rub all over with half the spicy butter mixture.

Fill the bottom of a steamer with water and bring to the boil.

Place the chicken legs in the top part of the steamer, above the boiling water.

Cover with a lid, reduce the heat and steam for 35–40 minutes until the legs are cooked and tender.

Meanwhile, preheat the grill (broiler).

Place the steamed chicken legs in the grill (broiler) pan and spread with the remaining spicy butter.

Grill (broil) until the surface of the chicken is lightly golden. Serve immediately.

PERFECT SIDES AND COMPLEMENTS

Whatever poultry dish I cook, I always find there are times when a special sauce, a great stuffing or a flavoured butter adds that something special, that finishing touch. Here are my favourite recipes for some butters, marinades, rubs, bastes, stuffings, sauces, chutneys and relishes that are sure to do just that. Each and every recipe is well worth the extra little bit of effort, if only because they're guaranteed to have family and friends asking for more.

Flavoured butters

These butters – also known as compound butters – are a combination of butter with flavourings and seasonings. The beauty of them is that they can be prepared in advance and kept refrigerated, or even frozen, until needed. When you use them with poultry – they work well with quail, guinea fowl or squab pigeon, as well as with chicken and poussins – simply spread the butter under the breast skin and all over the bird (see p.19). You can also use it under the skin when you're just cooking legs or breasts on their own, or put some on top of poultry portions when grilling (broiling). With their burst of flavour, these butters bring a whole new meaning to poultry.

Here are some of my favourites. If you want to make them into butter rolls, prepare the butter according to the recipe, then roll it in waxed paper into a sausage shape. Twist both ends of the paper tightly – it will look like a bonbon – and chill or freeze as required. To serve in slices, remove the butter from its paper, leave to soften for 2–3 minutes, then cut into 1cm (½in) slices.

PORCINI, HAZELNUT, THYME AND GARLIC BUTTER

Yield: enough for 2 roasting birds
75g (2½oz) dried porcini
2 tbsp ground and toasted hazelnuts
1 tbsp thyme leaves
2 garlic cloves, crushed
120g (scant 4½oz/½ cup) unsalted butter, chilled
Sea salt and freshly ground black pepper

Place the porcini in a coffee grinder or small blender and blitz to a fine powder. Transfer to a bowl and add the hazelnuts, thyme, garlic and salt and pepper. Beat in the butter until well amalgamated and use as required.

LEMON SAGE PESTO BUTTER

Yield: enough for 2 roasting birds
25g (scant 1oz/scant ½ cup) chopped sage leaves
25g (scant 1oz/¼ cup) grated Parmesan cheese
450g (1lb/3½ cups) pine nuts, toasted
1 garlic clove, crushed
Grated zest and juice of 1 lemon
2 tbsp olive oil
120g (scant 4½oz/½ cup) unsalted butter, chilled

Put the sage, Parmesan, pine nuts, garlic, lemon juice and zest in a coffee grinder or small blender. Add the olive oil and blitz to a smooth paste. Transfer to a bowl, then beat in the butter until well amalgamated. Use as required.

SUMMER HERB BUTTER

Yield: enough for 2 roasting birds
120g (scant 4½oz/½ cup) unsalted butter
10g (¼oz/scant ¼ cup) roughly chopped chives
15g (½oz/scant ¼ cup) tarragon leaves
10g (¼oz/ scant ¼ cup) parsley leaves
2 sprigs of thyme
Grated zest of ½ lemon
½ tsp sea salt

Put the butter in a coffee grinder or small blender and add the chives, tarragon, parsley, thyme, lemon zest and salt. Blitz to a smooth paste and use as required.

Marinades, rubs and bastes

These are simple ways of enhancing and adding extra flavour to your poultry. For the best possible results, it is important to prepare the bird properly. Make shallow, parallel cuts in the flesh with a small knife. The cuts will allow the flavour of the marinade, rub or baste to penetrate the meat, and will also make the finished dish look much more attractive.

Marinades

A plain piece of grilled (broiled) chicken can sometimes be a little bland, but marinating it before grilling (broiling) makes it far more exotic. As well as adding flavour, a marinade will help to tenderise the meat.

Since marinades generally contain some acidic ingredient, such as lemon, lime or orange juice, you should not marinate the poultry for longer than overnight, or the acid will react with the flesh and will effectively start to 'cook' it.

Either choose a china or glass dish for marinating the poultry. Aluminium is a definite no-no, as the combination of the acidic marinade and the metal can cause a chemical reaction that definitely won't do your meat any favours.

All these marinades are enough to marinate a large roasting bird or four poultry breasts.

SIMPLE OLIVE OIL, GARLIC AND LEMON MARINADE

100ml (3½fl oz/scant ½ cup) olive oil
6 garlic cloves, unpeeled and lightly crushed
1 lemon, unpeeled and thinly sliced

The day before, mix the ingredients together and pour over the poultry. Stir well to coat the poultry, then cover with clingfilm (plastic wrap) and put in the fridge to marinate overnight.

OLIVE OIL, LEMON, MUSTARD AND HERB MARINADE

4 tbsp olive oil
Juice and grated zest of 1 lemon
1 tsp Dijon mustard
1 tbsp oregano leaves
1 tbsp chopped flat-leaf parsley

The day before, mix the ingredients together and pour over the poultry. Stir well to coat the poultry, then cover with clingfilm (plastic wrap) and put in the fridge to marinate overnight.

ADOBO MARINADE

2 garlic cloves, crushed
1 tsp ground cumin
1 tsp dried oregano
1 tsp dried red chilli (red pepper) flakes
¼ tsp ground bay leaf
1 tsp ground black pepper
100ml (3½fl oz/scant ½ cup) orange juice
Juice of 1 lime

Place all the ingredients in a coffee grinder or small blender and blitz until smooth. Pour over the poultry. Stir well to coat the poultry, then marinate for 4 hours at room temperature.

GREEK YOGURT AND ROASTED GARLIC MARINADE

4 tbsp Greek-style natural yogurt

4 garlic cloves, roasted, then removed from their skins

1 tsp oregano

Juice of ½ lemon

1 tsp sea salt

The day before, place all the ingredients in a coffee grinder or small blender and blitz to a paste. Spread the paste over the poultry, then cover with clingfilm (plastic wrap) and put in the fridge to marinate overnight.

GOAT'S MILK SPICED YOGURT MARINADE

2 garlic cloves, crushed

½ tsp ground cumin

1 tbsp curry powder

½ tsp cayenne pepper

2cm (¾in) piece of root ginger, grated

½ tsp ground cinnamon

1 tsp sea salt

1 tsp freshly ground black pepper

100ml (3½fl oz/scant ½ cup) goat's milk yogurt or natural cow's milk yogurt

Place all the ingredients in a coffee grinder or small blender and blitz until smooth. Pour the marinade over the poultry. Stir well to coat the poultry, then marinate for 2 hours at room temperature.

SOUTH-EAST ASIAN MARINADE

1 tbsp ketchup manis (Indonesian sweet soy sauce)

½ tsp ground cinnamon

100ml (3½fl oz/scant ½ cup) lemon juice

2 stalks of lemongrass, tough outer layers removed and the rest finely chopped

2 garlic cloves, crushed

3 tbsp rice wine vinegar

5 star anise

The day before, put all the ingredients in a small pan over a medium heat. Bring to the boil, then reduce the heat and simmer for 5 minutes. Remove from the heat and leave to cool. Pour the marinade over the poultry. Stir well to coat the poultry, then cover with clingfilm (plastic wrap) and put in the fridge to marinate overnight.

CHEMOULA MARINADE

Pinch of fresh saffron strands

50g (1¾oz/1 cup) fresh coriander (cilantro), coarsely chopped

2 garlic cloves, crushed

¼ tsp smoked paprika (pimentón)

½ tbsp cumin seeds, toasted

Juice of ¼ lemon

1 tsp grated lemon zest

3 tbsp olive oil

Pinch of ground ginger

Sea salt and freshly ground black pepper

The day before, place the saffron in a mortar with the coriander (cilantro), garlic and a little salt. Add the paprika and cumin seeds, and pound to a paste. Stir in the lemon juice, zest and olive oil and season with pepper and ground ginger. Use to coat the poultry, then cover with clingfilm (plastic wrap) and put in the fridge to marinate overnight.

CLOVE HONEY, OREGANO AND MUSTARD MARINADE

1 onion, grated or finely chopped

2 garlic cloves, crushed

⅛ tsp red chilli powder

2 tbsp chopped oregano

6 tbsp olive oil

1 tbsp honey

½ tsp ground cloves

1 tbsp soft brown sugar

2 tbsp wholegrain mustard

The day before, place the onion, garlic, chilli, oregano and half the oil in a blender. Blitz to a paste. Spread the paste over the poultry, then cover with clingfilm (plastic wrap) and put in the fridge to marinate overnight.

The next day, mix the honey, cloves, sugar and mustard in a bowl. Remove the poultry from the marinade and brush the honey and mustard mixture liberally over it while it is being griddled or barbecued.

Rubs

Rubs are another useful addition to your poultry-cooking repertoire. They add extra pzazz with minimum effort.

A rub can be dry or wet. Dry rubs are simply mixtures of dry spices that are rubbed over the meat 1–2 hours before it is cooked, or even just before. The rub forms a tasty crust on the outside and helps to seal in the juices.

Wet rubs are dry rubs held together with a small amount of a moist ingredient such as oil or crushed garlic, or a condiment such as soy sauce, mustard or horseradish.

It is hard to say how much rub you need for any particular use – different cooks use different amounts. My suggestion is, just give them a try!

A FAVOURITE DRY RUB

2 tsp sea salt

1 tsp freshly ground black pepper

1 tsp cayenne pepper

1 tsp English mustard powder

6 tbsp dried oregano or thyme

4 bay leaves, crumbled

Mix the ingredients together and use as required.

SPICY TEXAS RUB

2 tbsp sweet paprika

1 tbsp chilli powder

1 tsp ground cumin

1 tsp ground coriander

1 tsp caster (superfine) sugar

1 tsp sea salt

½ tsp English mustard powder

1 tsp dried oregano

1 tsp medium curry powder

½ tsp cayenne pepper

Mix the ingredients together and use as required.

HORSERADISH AND CUMIN WET RUB

4 tbsp horseradish sauce (bought or homemade)

1 tbsp cumin seeds, lightly toasted

2 garlic cloves, crushed

3 tbsp olive oil

1 tsp sea salt

1 tsp freshly ground black pepper

Mix the ingredients together and use as required.

CHILLI COFFEE RUB

1 tbsp ground coffee (espresso if possible)

50g (1¾oz/¼ cup) soft brown sugar

¼ tsp chilli powder

¼ tsp ground cinnamon

1 tsp ground star anise

¼ tsp ground cumin

2 tbsp olive oil

Sea salt and freshly ground black pepper

Place the coffee, sugar, chilli powder, cinnamon, star anise and cumin in a coffee grinder or small blender and blitz to a fine powder. Rub all over the poultry. Place in a bowl, cover with clingfilm (plastic wrap) and leave to stand for 1 hour at room temperature. Before grilling (broiling) or griddling, season with salt and pepper, and brush with the olive oil.

Bastes

Basting poultry while it cooks helps to retain moisture, add flavour and give the poultry an attractive glazed appearance. All these bastes can be used when grilling (broiling), griddling or roasting any poultry. As with rubs, it is hard to specify how much you will need, so again, just give them a go.

CHINESE BARBECUE BASTE

3 tbsp dry sherry

100ml (3½fl oz/scant ½ cup) Chinese oyster sauce

2 tbsp clear honey

2 tbsp sweet chilli sauce

2 garlic cloves, crushed

2.5cm (1in) piece of root ginger, grated

1 tbsp chopped coriander (cilantro)

Mix all the ingredients together and use to baste the poultry as it cooks.

TOMATO, VINEGAR AND BROWN SUGAR BASTE

3 tbsp sherry vinegar

50g (1¾oz/¼ cup) soft brown sugar

2 garlic cloves, crushed

1 tsp cumin powder

1 tsp tomato purée (paste)

1 tbsp smoked paprika (pimentón)

Place the vinegar and sugar in a small pan over a medium heat. Cook for 5 minutes to make a light caramel. Add the garlic, cumin, tomato purée (paste) and smoked paprika. Cook for 2 minutes more. Use to baste the poultry as it cooks.

POMEGRANATE AND ORANGE MUSTARD BASTE

100ml (3½fl oz/scant ½ cup) concentrated orange juice

3 tbsp pomegranate molasses

2cm (¾in) piece of root ginger, grated

2 garlic cloves, crushed

1 tsp Dijon mustard

Place the orange juice in small pan over a medium heat. Bring to the boil and boil until it has reduced by half. Add the remaining ingredients and cook for 1 minute more. Use to baste the poultry as it cooks.

Stuffings

You can use prepared stuffings in two different ways: either stuffed inside the bird (see p.18), which means that the bird will take longer to cook, or cooked separately in a small roasting tin. Personally, this is the way I like to do my stuffing.

All these recipes provide enough stuffing for two large roasting birds.

CLASSIC SAGE AND ONION STUFFING

Sage and onion stuffing is traditionally English and is used for poultry as well as pork. I, like some other chefs, add a little grated apple to the recipe.

50g (1¾oz/3½ tbsp) unsalted butter

2 onions, finely chopped

250g (9oz/4½ cups) fresh fine white breadcrumbs

175g (6oz) good-quality pork sausage meat

Grated zest of 1 lemon

2 tbsp chopped sage

1 egg

200g (7oz) cooking apples, peeled and grated

Sea salt and freshly ground black pepper

Melt the butter in a large frying pan (skillet) over a medium heat. Add the onion and cook over a low heat for about 10 minutes until softened.

Transfer to a large bowl and leave to cool. Mix with the remaining ingredients and season with salt and pepper.

LEMON, ALMOND AND PARSLEY STUFFING

100g (3½oz/7 tbsp) unsalted butter

200g (7oz/3⅔ cups) fresh fine white breadcrumbs

Grated zest of 1 lemon

50g (1¾oz/⅓ cup) nibbed almonds

4 tbsp chopped flat-leaf parsley

1 tbsp thyme leaves

1 tsp chopped marjoram

Sea salt and freshly ground black pepper

Melt the butter in a frying pan (skillet) over a low heat. Add the breadcrumbs, lemon zest and almonds and cook for 4–5 minutes until the breadcrumbs are golden. Remove from the heat and transfer to a bowl to cool. Add the parsley, thyme and marjoram and season with salt and pepper.

ITALIAN PORCHETTA-STYLE STUFFING

2 tbsp olive oil

2 garlic cloves, crushed

1 red onion, finely chopped

2 celery sticks, finely chopped

1 carrot, finely chopped

1 tbsp thyme leaves

1 tbsp chopped sage

1 tbsp chopped flat-leaf parsley

1 tsp fennel seeds, toasted

1 cotechino sausage, skin removed and meat crumbled

120g (scant 4½oz) chicken livers, cleaned and diced

100ml (3½fl oz/scant ½ cup) dry white wine

100g (3½oz/generous 1¾ cups) fresh white breadcrumbs

Sea salt and freshly ground black pepper

Heat the oil in a frying pan (skillet) over a medium heat. Add the garlic, onion, celery, carrot, thyme, sage, parsley and fennel seeds. Cook for 6–8 minutes until the vegetables have softened but are not coloured.

Add the sausage meat and chicken livers, and cook over a medium heat for 10 minutes.

Add the wine and bring to the boil. Boil until the wine has reduced in volume by half. Transfer to a bowl and add the breadcrumbs. Mix well to bind the stuffing together. Season with salt and pepper.

TRADITIONAL CHESTNUT STUFFING

25g (scant 1oz/1¾ tbsp) unsalted butter

1 onion, finely chopped

3 tbsp chopped sage

200g (7oz) vacuum-packed chestnuts, chopped

1kg (2¼lb) good-quality pork sausage meat

2 eggs

100g (3½oz/generous 1¾ cups) fresh white breadcrumbs

¼ tsp ground allspice

Sea salt and freshly ground black pepper

Melt the butter in a frying pan (skillet) over a medium heat. Add the onion, sage and chestnuts. Cook for 10 minutes, or until the onions are soft. Transfer to a bowl and leave to cool. Add the sausage meat, eggs and breadcrumbs and mix well. Season with salt, pepper and allspice.

HAGGIS AND OATMEAL STUFFING

This is a stuffing with a Scottish twist. I adore haggis and its moistness makes it ideal to use as a stuffing for roast chicken or turkey. For a turkey, you need to double up the ingredients.

1 large onion, finely chopped
175g (6oz/2 cups) oatmeal (rolled oats)
75g (2½oz) shredded vegetable suet
300g (11oz) haggis, removed from its casing
Sea salt and freshly ground black pepper

Place the onion in a large bowl and add the oatmeal (rolled oats), suet and haggis. Mix well to combine, then season with salt and pepper.

JEWELLED COUSCOUS STUFFING

This stuffing with a Middle Eastern feel helps to make the poultry wonderfully moist. It is great with chicken, guinea fowl or squab pigeon.

300ml (10fl oz/1¼ cups) water
½ tsp saffron strands
200g (7oz/1 cup) couscous

50g (1¾oz/scant ⅓ cup) raisins, cooked in warm water until plump, then drained
75g (2½oz/½ cup) pistachios
25g (scant 1oz/scant ¼ cup) pine nuts, toasted
25g (scant 1oz/ ¼ cup) flaked almonds, toasted
Seeds of 1 pomegranate
¼ tsp ground turmeric
½ tsp ground cumin
Sea salt and freshly ground black pepper

Put the water in a pan and bring to the boil. Add the saffron, reduce the heat and simmer for 5 minutes.

Place the couscous in a dish, pour over the saffron water and cover with clingfilm (plastic wrap). Leave to steam for 5 minutes, then remove the clingfilm (plastic wrap) and fluff up with a fork. Add the raisins, pistachios, pine nuts, almonds and pomegranate seeds. Season with turmeric, cumin and salt and pepper. Leave to cool.

Sauces

A great sauce really adds value to any meat dish, and poultry is no exception. The following sauces are based on timeless classics: they are all truly delicious.

MULLED CRANBERRY SAUCE

This gorgeous cranberry sauce is flavoured with seasonal mulled wine and spices. It will keep for up to a week in the fridge. It is good with turkey, of course, and also with goose, duck and squab pigeon.

> Yield: 750ml (1¼ pints/25fl oz)
> 450g (1lb/4½ cups) cranberries (fresh or frozen)
> 1 Granny Smith apple, peeled, cored and diced
> 200ml (7fl oz/scant 1 cup) red wine
> 100ml (3½fl oz/scant ½ cup) port (any type wil do)
> 125g (4½oz/½ cup + 2 tbsp) caster (superfine) sugar
> Grated zest of 1 orange
> Grated zest of 1 lemon
> Good pinch of ground cloves
> 1 tsp ground cinnamon
> Pinch of English mustard powder
> 1 tsp cornflour (cornstarch)
> 1 tbsp water
> 2 tbsp redcurrant jelly
> Sea salt and freshly ground black pepper

Place the cranberries, apple, wine, port, sugar, orange and lemon zests, cloves and cinnamon in a pan over a medium heat. Cook for 12–15 minutes, stirring continuously, until the mixture has reduced and thickened.

Combine the mustard powder and cornflour (cornstarch) with the water. Stir into the cranberry mixture and add the redcurrant jelly. Reduce the heat and simmer for 2 minutes more. Season with sea salt and pepper. Leave to cool then refrigerate until ready to use.

OLD-FASHIONED APPLE SAUCE

Cooking apples add a touch of tartness to this traditional sauce that goes well with the poultry. This recipe dates back to the early eighteenth century. It is good with roast duck, goose and guinea fowl.

> Yield: 750ml (1¼ pints/25fl oz)
> 450g (1lb) cooking apples, peeled, cored and coarsely chopped
> 75ml (2½fl oz/⅔ cup) water

> Grated zest of ½ lemon
> 25g (scant 1oz/2 tbsp) caster (superfine) sugar
> 15g (½oz/1 tbsp) unsalted butter, chilled and cut into small pieces

Place the apples, water and lemon zest in a pan over a medium heat. Cover with a lid and bring to the boil. Reduce the heat and simmer gently for 10–12 minutes, or until the apples have softened and become pulpy in consistency.

Add the sugar and cook for 1 minute, then remove from the heat.

Stir in the butter and serve immediately. If you prefer a smoother sauce, add the butter then place in a small blender and blitz until smooth. Serve warm.

BREAD SAUCE

Bread sauce is the classic to serve with any poultry, although it is especially good with chicken and game. It is simple to prepare; the cream adds a lovely richness, while the addition of a little grated nutmeg or mace gives it an added spiciness.

> Yield: 750ml (1¼ pints/25fl oz)
> 1 onion, halved
> 4 cloves
> 600ml (1 pint/2½ cups) full-fat (whole) milk
> 1 small bay leaf
> 150g (5½oz/2¾ cups) fresh white breadcrumbs
> 60ml (2fl oz/¼ cup) double (heavy) cream
> 50g (1¾oz/3½ tbsp) unsalted butter, chilled and cut into small pieces
> Freshly ground nutmeg or mace
> Sea salt and freshly ground black pepper

Stud each onion half with 2 cloves. Place the milk, bay leaf and onion in pan over a medium heat. Bring to the boil, then remove from the heat and leave to infuse for 1 hour.

Strain the milk into a clean pan and return to the heat. When the milk is hot, add the breadcrumbs. Reduce the heat and cook for about 2 minutes over a low heat until thick.

Add the cream, stir in the butter and season to taste with nutmeg or mace and salt and pepper. Serve warm.

Chutneys and relishes

Chutney and relishes are a great accompaniment to most types of poultry and game. Not only that, but they are a great way to use up a glut of seasonal produce. The flavour of all good chutney is improved the longer the chutney is left to mature. Store in the fridge in a sealed jar, until ready for use.

GOOSEBERRY AND ELDERFLOWER CHUTNEY

This is a brilliant way to use fresh gooseberries during their short summer season. It is great with goose or duck as the acid in the chutney helps cut the fat in the bird.

Yield: 750ml (1¼ pints/25fl oz)

450g (1lb/3 cups) gooseberries (fresh or frozen)

1 onion, chopped

1 garlic clove, crushed

½ tsp English mustard powder

1 tbsp fresh lemon juice

200ml (7fl oz/scant 1 cup) white wine vinegar

100g (3½oz/scant ⅔ cup) raisins

175g (6oz/scant 1 cup) soft brown sugar

1 tbsp elderflower cordial

Sea salt

Place the gooseberries, onion, garlic, mustard powder and lemon juice in a pan over a medium heat. Add two-thirds of the vinegar and bring to the boil. Reduce the heat, then simmer for 30 minutes, stirring occasionally, until the mixture has thickened.

Add the raisins, sugar and remaining vinegar, and season with a little salt. Cook for about 30 minutes more over a low heat until the mixture is thick and syrupy.

Remove from the heat, stir in the elderflower cordial and leave to cool.

CRANBERRY AND PICKLED BEETROOT RELISH

This relish is especially tasty with roast turkey, duck or goose.

Yield: 750ml (1¼ pints/25fl oz)

300ml (10fl oz/1¼ cups) water

450g (1lb/4½ cups) cranberries (fresh or frozen)

100g (3½oz/½ cup) caster (superfine) sugar

1 Granny Smith apple, peeled and grated

2 tbsp stem (preserved) ginger, drained and finely chopped

4 tbsp white wine vinegar

225g (8oz) pickled beetroots, drained and cut into small cubes

3 tbsp redcurrant jelly

Place the water, cranberries, sugar, apple, stem (preserved) ginger and vinegar in a pan over a medium heat. Bring to the boil, then reduce the heat and simmer for 10–15 minutes, or until the mixture has thickened. Add the beetroot and redcurrant jelly and cook for 5 minutes more. Leave to cool. Serve at room temperature.

The perfect gravy

While your poultry or meat is roasting, it produces the two important components of gravy – the fat and the caramelised residue that is stuck to the bottom of the roasting tin. These, plus the stock you use, will determine the quality of the gravy you end up with. Ideally, use a good meat stock, though a stock cube will do the job, too.

To make the gravy, once the meat is cooked, remove it from the roasting tin and pour away all the fat from the tin except for about 1 tbsp.

To make a thin gravy, place the tin over a medium heat, then add approximately 600ml (1 pint/2½ cups) stock and bring to the boil. Scrape up any residue from the base of the pan, then boil briskly until the gravy has reduced by half. Check the seasoning, then strain the gravy through a fine sieve (strainer) and serve immediately.

For a thick gravy, stir 1 tbsp plain (all-purpose) flour into the fat left in the tin. You can add a little more if necessary; the idea is for the flour to absorb all the fat in the tin. Cook for 1 minute, or until the flour is lightly browned, then add approximately 600ml (1 pint/2½ cups) stock and bring to the boil. Cook for 5 minutes. Check the seasoning, then strain the gravy through a fine sieve (strainer) and serve immediately.

If you like, you can add a little port, Madeira or sherry to the gravy for added flavour.

thin gravy

thick gravy

Index

Acknowledgements

And now the moment has come to thank the many people who have worked with me on this book.
Lara King, who did a great job of typing my manuscript and making it readable.
Hilary Mandleberg, superb editor and friend. Working with you is a pleasure.
Lawrence Morton, for designing the book so beautifully.
Cynthia Inions, for her wonderful prop styling, as usual.

Photographer **Kevin Summers** and his fantastic team. Between them, they have helped to bring my recipes to life in colour.

And a special thanks to **Jacqui and her team**.
I deeply value your support, friendship and professionalism in helping to create some lovely books together. Thank you.